Dear Sandy:

You're a wonderful artist!
Best Wishes

Vince Manuel 3/23/11

We're friends off the field, but enemies on the field.

George Steinbrenner
New York Yankees

VINCE NAIMOLI

VINCE NAIMOLI

Business, Baseball & Beyond

STAR GROUP
INTERNATIONAL INC.

Published 2009

StarGroup International
West Palm Beach, Florida
561.547.0667
www.stargroupinternational.com

FIRST EDITION

Project coordinator: Brenda Star
Cover & book design: Mel Abfier
Writer: Linda Haase and Vince Naimoli
Editor: Libby Wells
Media coordinator: Andrew Ramdeholl

Printed in Korea

VINCE NAIMOLI - Business, Baseball & *Beyond*
ISBN 978-1-884886-93-5

Photos:

Robert Rogers, pages 64, 67, 68, 69, 70, 71, 72 (bottom), 73, 74, 75, 77, 78, 79, 81, 82, 83

Skip Milos. pages 90, 92, 96

Illustration, page 87, Todd Dawes, www.dawesart.com

Dedicated to my wife, Lenda,

my daughters, Christine, Tory, Alyson and Lindsey

and grandchildren, Jack, Matt, Will, Enzo and one yet to be named.

dedication

All proceeds from the sale of this book that are due the author
will go to private charities

contents

preface

Vince, Lenda and Governor Charlie Crist

CHARLIE CRIST
GOVERNOR

For most of the 20th century, Major League Baseball clubs have come to the Sunshine State every spring to prepare for the upcoming season. Going to Grapefruit League games was an opportunity to see our favorite players perform at close range. On some days, I was among those who took advantage of catching a couple of innings during the lunch hour.

The only sad part about spring training occurred at the end of March when the teams – all of the teams – would head north or west to begin the season. Florida tried for many years to get a team of its own. Finally, Major League Baseball awarded a team for Miami, which began play in 1993.

While I was personally pleased with this development, I agreed with the Tampa Bay community that we wanted one for this region. There were, to use a football term, a couple of false starts. Negotiations to bring the Chicago White Sox to Tampa Bay broke down and Baseball disapproved a signed agreement to bring the San Francisco Giants to St. Petersburg.

Finally, on March 9, 1995 the dream became a reality when Major League Baseball owners voted unanimously to award an expansion franchise to Tampa Bay. For those who relished having the World Series in St. Petersburg in 2008, and I enjoyed it as much as any fan, we owe Vince Naimoli a debt of gratitude.

To obtain an expansion franchise, Major League Baseball expected a rock-solid ownership group that included partners with local roots. Vince worked tirelessly with a team of investors that met all of the criteria and made it impossible to deny Florida its second franchise.

He was not alone, but his strong will and dedication to the cause of bringing Major League Baseball to Tampa Bay was infectious and ultimately led to the Devil Rays taking the field on March 31, 1998. With a professional football team, hockey team, and a nearby basketball team, this club made Tampa Bay a major league community.

Vince has been an outstanding contributor to the Tampa Bay community and a personal friend to me. As Chairman Emeritus and Founder of the Rays, his place in Tampa Bay baseball history will be forever secure. I thank him both for his role in bringing Major League Baseball to St. Petersburg and for his friendship through the years.

Sincerely,

Charlie Crist

Vince with Baseball Commissioner Bud Selig at a Notre Dame game

"Vince Naimoli is a baseball pioneer. Through his hard work, business skills, perseverance and leadership, he brought Major League Baseball to the Tampa Bay area. And, through those same traits and attributes, he helped build the franchise from scratch and helped turn it into the successful club it is today on the field of play.

"Vince is a good friend and was a trusted advisor and a staunch supporter during his time in baseball. As the Commissioner, I relied on Vince's business expertise and named him to Major League Baseball's Blue Ribbon Task

foreword

Force on Baseball Economics in 1999, a committee that helped transform baseball's economic landscape and brought competitive balance to the game.

"I have a great amount of respect for Vince. He has worked hard for everything he has achieved in life.

Allan H. (Bud) Selig
Baseball Commissioner

River running through Paterson, N.J.

The
Early
Years

Vince, Paterson, New Jersey, 1945

Growing up in Paterson, New Jersey

I WOUND UP MY ARM, READY TO LET FLY THE *PATERSON EVENING TIMES* I DELIVERED IN THE AFTERNOONS. THE PORTABLE RADIO TUCKED PRECARIOUSLY UNDER MY OTHER ARM WAS CRACKLING, AND I STRAINED TO HEAR THE DODGERS-GIANTS GAME AS I PEDALED MY RED SCHWINN FLEETWOOD FLYER THROUGH DOWNTOWN.

My paper route netted me three cents per customer a week, and to sweeten the pot I started selling Christmas and Easter cards along the way. A lot of my customers liked to peruse those fancy New York papers, too, so I bought them at city hall, then tacked on a couple of cents for a delivery fee. When I started my business I tossed about

40 papers, but I'm a go-getter and before long I had 150 customers.

Delivering papers could have been tedious, but I broke the boredom by announcing my arrival with the brrrrrr, brrrrrr, brrrrrrrrr reverberating from the baseball card flapping against the spokes of the back wheel of my bicycle. That sound was my calling card. Now, I wish I hadn't sacrificed those venerable old cards, which were reduced to shredded bits of paper. They'd probably be worth a fortune today.

Baseball glove, c. 1930s

Nearly all my customers had a business. One man made great slipcovers, but needed help getting the word out. Back then, putting ads on car windshields was a novel idea, so when I wasn't delivering papers or playing pinball, I spent hours in a parking lot at one of the first outdoor malls in East Paterson, N.J., lifting up windshield wipers and tucking advertising fliers underneath. I probably made a penny for every 10 ads. It was a lot of money at the time, especially for a kid.

I grew up in Paterson, N.J., dubbed The Silk City, which sounds a lot more glamorous than it was. The mills that created sumptuous soft silk had declined by the time I was born in 1937. But it didn't matter. In our diminutive house perched on the side of a hill, a stone's throw from the railroad tracks, there wasn't any money for fancy cloth.

My younger brother, Raymond, and I shared a room, and a bed, in the minuscule third-floor attic Dad had converted to a bedroom. Ray was a restless sleeper, always kicking me in the shins and the back. Sometimes I can still feel those gangly feet waking me in the middle of the night.

There wasn't room to tack posters or photos on the walls, but our window offered a panoramic view of the railroad tracks and the mesmerizing freight trains lugging 100 rumbling cars as they snaked around the curve in the mountain.

Vince, 5 years old

We eventually got used to the train's thump, thump, thump, shrill whistle and intense headlight which lit up our third-floor room like a bolt of lightning every night as we were drifting off to sleep.

The locomotive that provided the soundtrack for our dreams wasn't nearly as exhilarating to watch, however, as was the Lionel train set that was our only substantial Christmas toy. Raymond and I would sprawl on the floor for hours, arranging the cars just so on the figure-eight track. We'd argue over whose turn it was to press the

button that propelled it on its journey, squealing with delight as we imagined ourselves jumping aboard for the ultimate adventure.

Who knows how my parents were able to afford our prized possession. But we never tired of it. It's a good thing, because we didn't get many Christmas presents. Well, there were gifts but we didn't get to play with them much—they were stored away to be recycled and given at Christmas again the following year. I guess I did get to enjoy them eventually, I still have a pair of boxing gloves I got one year.

Vince, Central High School, Paterson, N.J., 1955

But we didn't mind living modestly. We didn't know any other life. We had no idea we were poor. We were just happy, carefree kids. But we always had enough to eat, thanks to my Italian-born grandfather who was a butcher and my mother who was a fine cook. I don't think I ever had a bad meal. In the morning, the tantalizing aroma of salty, succulent Taylor ham would waft up the stairs and roust me out of bed and downstairs to the kitchen faster than those locomotives that roared past our house.

We were a close-knit family. My grandparents lived next door, sharing a house with my Aunt Sarah and Uncle Albert and their kids. Aunt Sue and Uncle Walter lived two doors down, which was perfect because their daughter, Mary Ann, and I were close.

My Aunt Jean (I called her Geech, because I couldn't pronounce Jean) lived on the first floor of our house. Jean was one-of-a-kind. She loved to iron and would press our socks, underwear and T-shirts. She was a nurse, but at one time toiled at a Laundromat and she must have missed the clean, spring-air scent of clothes fresh out of the dryer. I was impressed, but not enough to stick around for ironing lessons.

Central High School, Paterson, N.J., 1955

It was easy to escape to my grandparents' house, stopping to tug figs off their tree and stuffing them in my mouth, marveling at the peach/strawberry flavor that burst from them. I missed that tree in the winter, when my grandfather wrapped it up to protect it against the blistering cold air. My grandparents, mother and father,

Graduation Exercises

PUBLIC SCH[OOL]
PATERSON, NEW [JERSEY]

CLASS OF JANUARY
1955

COMMENCEMENT

Central High School

MANLEY HALL
WEDNESDAY EVENING
JANUARY 26, 1955

To Vince
Best Wishes
and Luck
in the future
Joan

Vince
Good Luck to a
wonderful Guy. It's
been fun going through
Grammer and High
School with you.
Bunny

Vince
Lots of luck
& best wishes
to a swell guy
Jack

Joan Neuberger

"Jo"—Commercial

A wisp of a miss . . . enjoys eating and bowling . . . seen with Dorothea . . . dislikes to do homework on week-ends . . . "How cute!" . . . plans to be a bookkeeper.

Vincent Naimoli

"Vince"—Academic

Always full of high ambition . . . enjoys playing ball . . . usually seen with the boys . . . dislikes cars that cut in and out . . . "I'll clue you!" . . . plans to be an electrical engineer.

Lavinia Mitchell

"Bunny"—Commercial

Bewitching smile and voice . . . enjoys singing and eating . . . seen with Joyce and Marie . . . dislikes waiting for buses . . . "The kid's a comedian!" . . . hopes to be a successful singer.

Vince Much [L?]

Rose Palatucci

"Roe"—Commercial

Her smile reflects her personality . . . enjoys being with that guy . . . seen with "Liz" and Ruth . . . dislikes homework . . . "Oh boy!" . . . plans to be happily married.

Cap and Gown Committee
Co-chairmen:
[H]elene Malone and Angelo Martucci

Ticket Committee
Co-chairmen:
Diane Collins and Vince Naimoli

Central High School, 1955-1959

Mary Ann, my brother Ray, and all my aunts and uncles are deceased. I hope they rest in peace.

Ebbets Field, home of the Brooklyn Dodgers

My brother and I spent nearly every second we could outside. That's where our cat, Snowball, lived, but outdoor felines are lured by all kinds of foul-smelling trouble, so he became known as Stinky.

The all-important 107-mile Morris Canal, which transported anthracite and silk from the late 1820s to the 1920s, had dried up. So we dragged jugs to the nearby mountain and filled them with clear, sparkling spring water so icy it numbed our fingers.

We walked everywhere, including to school because school buses didn't exist in our area. I thought I was the luckiest kid in the world when I scraped up a few cents to buy a ticket to ride the public bus that stopped near my school. I'd dash toward a window seat and daydream as the world went by during the mile-long ride to school.

Where I lived, baseball was an all-consuming fever. It seemed like there were three types of people in my world: Yankees fans, Giants fans and Dodgers fans. My ardent worship of the Dodgers came naturally. My dad was from Brooklyn and his dad (my paternal grandfather), a jeweler who emigrated from Italy in the 1890s, lived there. As far as I was concerned, the Dodgers' 5-foot-11 inch, 204-pound Jackie Robinson could outplay anyone. Not only was he a great athlete, he was the first player to break the color barrier that segregated Major League Baseball for five decades. (Years later, I named my suite at Tropicana Field for Jackie Robinson.) Besides, the Dodgers were the underdog and I liked rooting for the underdogs of the world.

When I was 10, the Yankees dominated baseball and captured the World Series in an action-packed seven-game series against my beleaguered Brooklyn Dodgers. It was 1947, Robinson's first year in the league. The cry went out: "Wait till next year!" I couldn't wait.

Vince's award for lettering in football

But it broke my heart four years later when Bobby Thomson hit the game-winning home run in a Dodgers/Giants playoff game, snatching the 1951 National League pennant from us. That homer, hit off pitcher Ralph Branca's fastball, turned what seemed like certain defeat for the Giants into a 5-4 victory. The home run was forever known as the shot heard round the world, but my scream of agony was probably just as loud.

Victory was sweet, though, in 1955 when the Dodgers, those "bums from Brooklyn" won their first World Series title 4-3 against the all-powerful Yankees. Three years later, the baseball roller coaster ride crashed and burned when the Dodgers were "hijacked" (in my opinion) to the West coast. I gave up watching baseball for 15 years after that and it still hurts when I think of that desertion.

Sports were supreme in my life. We played baseball, basketball and football.

Commemorative baseball pennant

It didn't matter if there was a torrential rainstorm or triple-digit temperatures, we played baseball from 9 a.m. to 4 p.m. most summer days. Our pitcher had astonishing speed but no control. He would strike out 35 batters but walk 50. It was a long game.

Of course, we hiked the three miles to the field, stopping to skip rocks at the lake. There was no money for lunch or drinks; we were grateful for a sip from a water fountain, even when it was lukewarm and left sand in our mouths.

It was a great day when we could convince a sponsor to give us uniforms and equipment. Most of the time we begged, borrowed, and yes, sometimes even stole what we needed.

I couldn't hit the ball worth a darn, but I was the manager of the team, so I put myself on first base. I figured if I couldn't send the ball whizzing past my opponents' reach, I'd use my strategizing skills to propel the team to victory. And it worked. We even won the league once. Put the right people in the right positions and you'd be amazed at what you can accomplish. Of course, luck plays a part in winning, too, but I learned that much later.

Central High School, Paterson, N.J.

I may have day-dreamed about fans screaming my name as I closed in on a triple play or hit a homerun, but I never imagined I'd own a baseball team one day. Actually, I never had a plan for my life at all. But I learned the most important thing in my life early: Working hard is essential; you don't need money to get ahead. Just hard work, grit, perseverance, tenacity and a bit of luck. Like Coach Lou Holtz always says, luck is where timing and preparation meet.

Even today, when people ask what I do for fun, I tell them: "I work." Give it up, they implore. "Someone has to do it," I tell them, knowing I'm not about to alter my 6 a.m. to 6 p.m. daily work schedule anytime soon. I failed at retirement. Twice. The third time would not be the charm, at least not for me.

Expectations were high in our house. My mom, Margaret (though everyone called her Peggy), had a subtle way of encouraging me to do better, to strive higher. She did it in a nice way, the way she did everything. Nearly every down-and-out person in Paterson knew that if they knocked on our door, Mom would welcome them with a smile, a homemade sandwich and a kind word.

My dad, Ralph, a second-generation immigrant, worked in a subway. At night, he and Mom would sit across from each other and she'd quiz him so he could pass the test to become a stationary engineer and get a better job in a boiler room. I didn't know it then, but engineering was to be part of my destiny. When I entered the hallowed halls of Notre Dame it was the only major I'd consider. I wish Dad and Mom could have lived to hear that the National Association of Power Engineers recognized him as an honorary member. That'd make them beam!

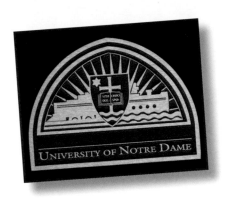

Dad was quiet and soft-spoken and spent his free time in a dilapidated workroom he built in our front yard. When it came time to make the props for the play Robin Hood, which I produced and directed at my grammar school one year, it was a good thing he had all those tools. He was also a whiz at fixing plumbing and electrical problems. I went with him on jobs, but did more daydreaming then paying attention. Now, I wish I'd watched him more carefully and learned more.

No matter how weary Dad felt after a long day of work, he'd stop at Dr. Levinson's house and fix anything that was broken. That's how he paid our doctor bills, which is a good thing because I had asthma when I was a kid and there was no health insurance then.

Dad always hoped that a major road would come through and some rich developer would buy our house. Route 80 did become a reality, but that was after he sold the house. He probably wouldn't have gotten much for our little house, but still… one could dream.

My evening escape was listening to sports and the cowboy exploits of Tom Mix on the radio. I'd settle down every night at 5:30, engrossed by the Ralston Straight Shooters Club, which urged us to "shoot straight and be honest."

That was good advice, and maybe I was thinking about it when I entered the radio station's contest to name Tom Mix's dog. I imagined the prize, a red, black and white genuine Mickey Mouse watch, wrapped

Tom Mix, c.1940s

securely around my wrist. Too many years have passed for me to remember why the name Buckwing came to mind, but I mailed in my suggestion, and like any kid, went about my life.

Months later, I was outside playing, when Mom ran down the hill, waving the letter announcing my win in one hand and the coveted watch in the other. "You won! you won!" she said, beaming.

I loved that watch, but I didn't wear it much after Uncle Lou gave me an incredible Bulova when I got my high school diploma. And there was certainly no place for it on my arm after Uncle Tony bestowed on me a lavish Lucien Piccard watch when I graduated Notre Dame.

The Mickey Mouse watch was a treasure though, and always reminded me of those precious carefree days of childhood. My friends and I didn't realize all the implications of growing up during the tumultuous war years.

I was too young to understand what had happened on December 7, 1941, but I remember it vividly: It was my Aunt Sue's birthday and the party was just getting started. The kitchen table was pushed to the side and the radio was on a shelf, tuned to a station playing the best swing music, sure signs that they'd be cutting the rug till all hours.

Mickey Mouse watch, c.1940s

But instead of the Glenn Miller Orchestra's lively 'Chattanooga Choo Choo,' we were stunned into silence by the devastating news that Pearl Harbor had been bombed. President Franklin D. Roosevelt proclaimed the day as "a date which will live in infamy." My aunt probably remembered it every year for another reason: We never had a birthday party for her again.

I kept busy during my school years and never

had trouble finding ways to amuse myself. I was a straight-A student, a member of the National Honor Society, the high school yearbook staff and of various sports teams as well as class vice president and a stringer for the local paper. But I liked to kick it up a bit, too.

Big Band era, c.1940s

I f my parents thought I'd graduate from Central High School without a blemish, I disappointed them. If they'd measured my mischievous streak, it would have been longer than the Hudson River. And it sure got me in trouble the day the assistant principal discovered me eating lunch standing up in the cafeteria. "Sit down!" he bellowed. Gee, I thought, what was wrong with him? Couldn't he see that there was no place to sit? So, I did what any wisenheimer worth his salt would do: I pulled the chair out from under some kid and plopped into his seat. That stunt earned me a trip to the principal's office, but I escaped with a warning. Years later, I realized I'd gotten off too easily.

I wasn't so fortunate when Mom discovered my secret life as a football player. I thought I had a fool-proof scheme. I'd convinced her that I had to attend every one of my high school's football games and practices to collect fodder for my sports report in the *Paterson Evening Times*.

I wrote reports, darned good ones (I thought) and I did it gratis. Mom thought I was industrious and benevolent. I was smug, chuckling to myself about how volunteering to be a stringer had provided the perfect alibi for me to play football, which Mom forbade, declaring it a dangerous sport and warning that I'd probably get hurt.

Bobble head, c.1940s

I had the perfect ruse: We kept our gear at the stadium so Mom never saw my red and black Paterson Colts football uniform. My carefully thought-out scheme worked for a while, until the day I limped home after a grueling practice. "I'm OK Mom," I told her anxiously while trying to divert her attention. "I just tripped."

The thought of coming clean never entered my mind. I thought I was infallible. But who could have foreseen the improbable event that resulted in my most glorious moment on the football field being the downfall of my deception?

In those days, I'm not sure they had the means to measure adrenaline levels like NASA did with the astronauts while they were hurtling between here and the moon. But if they could have tracked my adrenaline the day I was playing defense, pursuing an All-State player from a school in East Rutherford, N.J., who was rushing to the 10-yard line, it would have made history.

I dashed up behind him, flying so fast the wind was flapping under the #38 on my jersey. The next thing I knew, he was sprawled on the grass and the football was free. Fumble! My first instinct was to dive on it and hold position. But the opportunity was there to do more, and when I looked at that open green field, I couldn't resist scooping up the ball and making a run for the faraway goal line.

With a whole lot of the wrong-colored jerseys in hot pursuit, I'm not sure how I covered 90 yards without someone tackling me, but my teammates reacted quickly to take out the fastest of our opponents and I huffed down the field to one of the sweetest touchdowns of my career.

There's nothing that feels as good in a football game as scoring a touchdown, and for a guy playing defense, you can multiply that by 10.

I was gasping for breath, but I was breathing, so who cared? It's events like this that remain in your memory long after your playing days, that moment of glory when you've lifted your teammates and your school to a victory.

But, I didn't realize the sports editor of the paper was watching the game, whooping and hollering in the stands, dumbfounded when he saw a defensive end charging to the goalpost with the ball. I did my usual write-up of the game, making sure I left my name out. But the editor was so impressed with my performance he rewrote it, glorifying every tidbit of the play.

Now my mother was not going to miss hearing about something that was displayed prominently in the local newspaper. And if she hadn't seen it, her friends would make sure she knew.

There were thousands of copies of the damning evidence all over town, proof that I was not just keeping stats for the football team but was, in fact, contributing some of them. I knew I'd disappointed her, and made her angrier than I had ever seen her. But it was a pretty dramatic way to get caught! How many kids can say their falsehoods were exposed in the newspaper?

But since it was my senior year and we had only one more game to play, I got to finish the season.

Years later, her prediction about getting hurt came true. My brother, Ray, was injured in a dramatic play that broke his nose and deviated his septum. His pride may have been hurt even more, but the ultimate loss, at least as far as Mom was concerned, was him losing his football scholarship to the U.S. Air Force Academy after failing the physical because the break affected his breathing.

Mom was right (again), people did get hurt playing football, but the injury didn't spoil his future. He ended up graduating from Notre Dame and having a successful career as an accountant and CFO for several prominent companies. The last 15 years of his life were spent as our trusted CFO for the Tampa Bay Rays. His contributions were indispensable; he always came up with solutions for tough challenges.

I turned out pretty decent, too, partly because I learned early not to settle for second best. That lesson, like many others, was learned on the football field. Coach Kerns had a habit of putting me on the team's second string. I grew tired of the slight.

"Hey Coach. How come I don't get to start?" I asked. "Because you never ask," he replied. I started every game after that. I learned: Ask and you shall receive. Well, at least some of the time. But it never hurts to ask.

When I was 12, there was a big change in our household. The twins, Alan and Jill, were born. I adored them and when I left for college five years later, I missed them terribly.

They were in kindergarten, I was at Notre Dame, away from my family and all that was familiar. I did, however, keep one thing constant: I was still playing football and studying. Classes were sacred, but so was football. My drafting class, which I thought I excelled in, happened to coincide with many practices. Football triumphed and I cut class one time too many and got a C.

I had been an excellent draftsman in high school and even worked for the city of Paterson doing drafting. I decided that academics needed to take precedent, so I shifted football to the sidelines. Instead, I coached intramural teams and they did pretty well.

At one point, a group of former West Point football players transferred to Notre Dame and formed an off-campus football team

New York City subway, c. 1940s

Vince's report card

that went undefeated. The team I coached (which had two players that later played on Notre Dame's varsity football team and went on to pro ball and a third player who played pro ball in Canada), played the West Point transferees in the league's championship game in Notre Dame's stadium and beat them. That was a sweet victory.

But mostly, I studied, even on the one "snow day," when we were dismissed from class after 29 inches of snow fell in three hours.

Sure, I could have been tossing snowballs, sledding or making snowmen, but I was there on an Navy ROTC scholarship and was so grateful that I didn't want to let anyone down, especially Mom, who was so proud when my picture was splashed on the front of the paper announcing my good fortune. "Local newspaper carrier makes good," the headline blared. I think I got the second-highest grade in the country on the NROTC scholarship test.

Too bad my high school guidance counselor didn't know how smart I was. When I told him I wanted to go to Notre Dame, he had four words for me: "You'll never get in."

Mr. Costello, the owner of a local plumbing supply store and a Notre Dame grad, was more encouraging. "You have good grades, you can do it," he told me. But, still, I worried. Joe Abbott, the human resource director of Hoffman LaRoche in Nutley, N.J. and another Notre Dame grad, was anxious to see me attend his alma mater since I was on an academic scholarship and was a reasonably good football player.

At the time, Notre Dame had reduced the number of football scholarships it was awarding and was looking for students who were good football players, but could pay for their schooling or were eligible for an academic scholarship. I qualified because I had an academic scholarship and was a decent football player.

I desperately needed a scholarship. I thought about going to a local college, but realized that the only part of my education I could afford was the train fare there. And the U.S. Navy came through for me, which is one reason I have always been indebted to the military.

While I was a freshman in NROTC at Notre Dame, I was nominated to take the competitive exam for the U.S. Naval Academy. Since the test had to be taken in my home district and I had never been on an airplane, I jumped at the opportunity. I scored eighth in the country on the exam and got the appointment. But I turned it down because I liked Notre Dame very much and didn't want to give up a year of college.

I wasn't surprised when I was accepted to the University of Pennsylvania on a fellowship to pursue my master's degree in mechanical engineering. I thought the reference from one of my advisors, a Notre Dame thermodynamics professor, would increase my chances of being accepted. I thought he was impressed with my studious ways, my determination and my intelligence, so I asked him to provide a reference, counting on a stellar letter of recommendation. But I was wrong. "This is the worst reference I've ever read," the dean of University of Pennsylvania's Morse School of Engineering told me.

I decided not to go to that university, but it all turned out OK. I got good grades at the other universities I attended, and I demonstrated that you can't always believe everything you read.

I kept my nose to the grindstone for the most part, but, occasionally my mischief got the best of me. I got in trouble again while pursuing an MBA at Fairleigh Dickinson University. The Money and Banking class professor was a know-it-all, and I thought I'd reciprocate by being a smart-aleck. I clamored to a seat in front, then persistently interrupted his presentations. He never yelled at me, which baffled me.

He got his revenge: I got a C in the class and graduated magna cum laude instead of summa cum laude and learned a valuable lesson: never show up those in authority. Years later, I got the last word. I was given the Fairleigh Dickinson University Outstanding Alumnus Award.

The twists and turns of my life were just beginning.

The
Corporate
Years

Collage given to Vince when Anchor Glass was listed on the New York Stock Exchange

The view from above

"IF YOU CAN REMEMBER ANYTHING ABOUT THE '60S, THEN YOU WEREN'T REALLY THERE," SCOFFED JEFFERSON AIRPLANE CO-FOUNDER PAUL KANTNER.

I was there, but I didn't don bell bottoms and granny glasses or listen to psychedelic music. While others burned flags, banished bras and reveled in sex, drugs and rock 'n' roll, I worked long hours during the day, plowed through graduate school at night and, with the help of my Dad, my Uncle Sam, who was a carpenter, and my brother, Raymond, built my house in Wyckoff, N.J. I was also starting my first family. Party time was for the rest of the world. I had another focus.

Vince cuts ribbon at new Anchor Glass facility

Looking back on my 35 years of corporate life, I have no regrets and wouldn't change anything. My philosophy was simple: I always aspired to a higher job. I knew if I worked hard and accomplished what people wanted me to achieve, I'd get that job.

For me, work is fun. You're never paid enough for what you do, so you'd better enjoy your job. Some people want to be millionaires, others want to retire at 50. I wanted to be president of a stock-exchange listed company. And when that happened, I wanted to be the CEO. The ladder was never high enough.

Even today, despite the exhilaration of the business of baseball, I miss the corporate life, especially turning around fallen-from-grace companies.

My first "real job" was at RCA, where we tried meticulously to perfect video tape recorders. We were on the cutting edge of technology, which made up for the seemingly paltry $542 monthly salary in the '60s.

It had been awhile since my high school days, but I ran into former classmates in the strangest places. It happened one day while I was at Mass at the U.S. Marine

Corps basic school base in Quantico, Virginia. As I was looking around, I saw 6-foot-tall Manfred "Shorty" Schwarz sitting in one of the pews. "Hey Shorty!" I said incredulously, wondering what he was doing in a Catholic church since I knew he was a non-Catholic. "What are you doing here?" Shorty, who later retired as a Marine Corps Colonel, retorted, "It's the only place I can get some rest."

I was also assigned to design a mobile radar for the U.S. Marine Corps. My orders were to design and make sure the AN-UPS1 radar could be set up in 30 minutes. For my colleague and I the set up was a cinch, a step above erecting a Lego structure. But no one could replicate it so our work was for naught.

I had a lot of cutting-edge jobs, including one at Reaction Motors, where we

Vince and Lenda at new Anchor Glass facility

One of Anchor Glass' plants

BOTTLER
Mid-Continent

JUNE-JULY, 1984

In This Issue
New Major Glass Supplier
SunRise Bottlers
Move Into Aseptics
State Convention Reports from
Arkansas, Illinois, Indiana, Kansas, Kentucky, Louisiana, Missouri, Oklahoma

worked on perfecting a liquid-propelled shoulder-held rocket engine for the Marines. The testing took place in the hinterlands of New Jersey. When we had almost finished the job, I discovered that the propellant, di-methyl hydrazine, was poisonous.

But who had time to ponder the ramifications? I was so busy in those days, I dashed out of work and scrambled to get to the New Jersey Institute of Technology, where I spent evenings pursuing my master's in mechanical engineering.

There was precious little time to spend with my darling daughter, Christine, who was born in 1961. (She's an Arizona State graduate and freelance communications specialist in Los Angeles who donates a lot of time to charity and also works for "the dog whisperer" Cesar Millan. A longtime pet lover, she adopted a stray dog that jumped in her car).

In the early '60s, I graduated from NJIT, then pursued an MBA at nights at Farleigh Dickinson University, while I was working and still building my house.

I borrowed $8,000 from my aunt for the land and another $16,000 from a local bank for materials to build a 3-bedroom, 2-bath ranch house on Hickory Hill Road. In essence, it was a 100 percent construction loan. I subcontracted a small grading job to a former high school colleague. As I talked to him, I realized he had a successful business and had accomplished it without a college degree, which made me wonder if I was wasting my time at night going to school. But, I realized later on, the degrees I worked so hard for were essential.

The house was on a hill, which created all kinds of problems. It was grueling

May 8, 1999

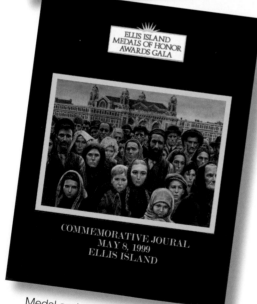

Medal and commemorative journal presented to medal recipients

work but we were a family who believed in hard work, so we gave it our all. The challenges were myriad, but it was the embankment that was the biggest obstacle. I didn't have the money to shore it up, so we came up with an idea that sounded good at the time.

The railroad had some abandoned ties that were free for the taking so we rented a truck to haul them away. We were hustling, trying to finish before the sun went down. Then my brother suddenly stopped. "Wait a minute, what's that?" he asked, pointing down the tracks. "Oh, no. It's a light on the front of a train. We have to get the truck off the tracks right now!"

He jumped in the truck and started the engine. It stalled. He was panicking and probably flooded it. With each excruciating turn of the key, my stomach turned, too. After a few scary moments, the truck revved and what a sweet sound it was. That was a story we never tired of telling.

Ellis Island Medal of Honor, 1999

Vince, and Reunion Co-Chairman, Joe Mulligan, present Class gift to Rev. John I. Jenkins, C.S.C., President, Notre Dame University

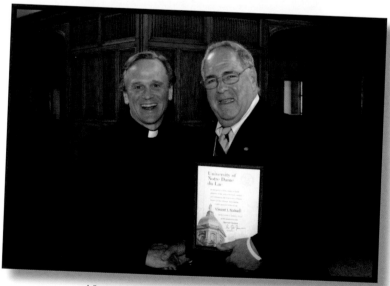

Vince, with Rev. John I. Jenkins, C.S.C.

The 2,000-square-foot house turned out to be a fine residence, even though the basement flooded nearly every time it rained until I put in a sump pump. To save money, I left the inside ceiling beams exposed, which made it unique. To me, the most important thing was having a house that was mine. I feel that the role of a father is to be a provider; having a house was crucial to my success in that arena.

It was a palace, made even grander because we could move in before my second daughter, Tory, was born in 1964, the same year I graduated from Fairleigh Dickinson University. (She's a Stephens College and Kellogg Graduate

School alumna and successful vice president of MasterCard, who lives in Illinois with her husband and three sons.)

When she was born, I was home baby-sitting Christine. When I got the call, I mouthed the words "it's a boy." But no, I was told, it's a girl. I wanted a boy, but Tory was so wonderful it didn't matter. I never did have a son, but I do have four terrific grandsons and one more grandson on the way.

Christine and Tory's childhood was like mine in that they were relatively poor but didn't really realize it. When I saw ads for the grand opening of Disney World in 1971, I regretted not having money for a plane ticket so they could be one of the first to get a kiss from Mickey Mouse. They went years later, when I moved to Florida, but they were much older then and the magic wasn't the same.

Lenda and Glenda

Vince, with wife, Lenda and daughter, Lindsey

Top: Christine
Middle: Alyson, Lindsey & Tory
Bottom: Vince with grandchildren, Matt, Jack, Enzo & Will

My tenacity and youthful can-do spirit served me well at American Cyanamid, a multibillion- dollar chemical and pharmaceutical company, where I was an assistant project engineer in the engineering and construction division.

When I was asked to drive to our plant in Michigan City, Indiana, in a blinding snowstorm, I said "no problem." It was a dangerous and stupid thing to do, but when you are young you think you are indestructible. When I arrived, I called my superiors. "I'm here," I taunted "where are you guys?"

The job was great, but I was aggressive and impatient. While assigned to the commercial development group during a cross-training stint, I worked for a man I thought was brilliant. But he was 40 and still an assistant manager. If he's so smart and competent and still an assistant manager, I mused, I'll never get ahead. So when I got a call from a

Certificate presented to Anchor Glass when listed on the New York Stock Exchange

head hunter saying the prestigious Continental Can Company (CCC) needed "leaders of the future," it was a turning point for me. I was ready to start work before I got off the phone.

We ultimately bid a sad farewell to the house on Hickory Hill Road and

Tampa Tribune, 1989

moved to Rochester, N.Y. in 1968. I found out soon after that the assistant manager at Cyanamid had been promoted and then shortly thereafter was made CEO of the company. But I had moved on and had no regrets.

At CCC, I was a lowly engineer trying to get a plant built in Weirton, West Virginia, and was running into all kinds of hassles. I needed cranes and I needed them fast. So I called one of the honchos at Weirton Steel and demanded he let us use their cranes. Word got back to my supervisors, who admonished me but admired my determination. I got the plant built and got a promotion, to boot.

While I was there I picked up a lot of cost-cutting ideas from a crusty manager who trained me. "Use scrap paper," he said, and from that day, I've never used anything else. I have a drawer full of scrap paper. I use the back of an envelope, a used piece of paper, anything that's surplus. It drives my secretaries nuts because they have to type letters from these tidbits. Not to mention the fact that my handwriting and printing look like an EKG reading.

I've always been practical and believe there's a solution to every problem. When an industrial engineer who was stuck in our Syracuse plant during one of the worst snowstorms in history called to tell me he ran out of money for the vending machine and was starving, I told him to take an ax and smash the machine. Problem solved.

In 1974, Alyson, who would follow in my footsteps at Notre Dame, was born. (She lives in Illinois with her husband, has one child and is expecting her second.) At Notre Dame, she was lucky enough to be mentored by Dr. Emil T. Hoffman, who was from Paterson, N.J., and had been my advisor at Notre Dame.

Not only was Dr. Hoffman a sought-after advisor, he was an excellent cook and would invite a group of students from northern Jersey to his house for Thanksgiving. We couldn't afford to go home so we were grateful we didn't

Vince, speaking at Annual Stockholders meeting

have to eat at the college dining hall, where the food often tasted like it was cooked in rancid grease. (One time a group of pranksters took a plate of really tough steaks and left them outside the dining hall manager's door.)

When I got a call from Dr. Hoffman one day about Alyson, I thought he was calling to praise her. But that wasn't the case. "Alyson is not doing well. She is in danger in a couple of subjects," he told me. I was perplexed - she had been tops in her class in a rigorous high school and was one of the elite chosen to attend Notre Dame.

But her heart wasn't in college, so she took a year off and worked in the inner city of Chicago which showed her how lucky she was to have what she had. She returned to Notre Dame and did very well. Afterward, she went to Ecuador for a year and taught English at a Catholic orphanage for girls.

When she returned, she got her masters in library science at the University of Illinois; she's still involved in teaching children at a library. I'm very proud of what Alyson has done with her life.

I stayed at Continental Can eight years. There was a lot of opportunity there and I took advantage of it all. I was a vice president of six operating divisions, the vice president of the food division (part of the marketing group) and general manager of production planning, among other positions.

I was even given a choice of a White House fellowship or attending Harvard Business School at the company's expense. I chose Harvard because many of my Notre Dame classmates had attended the school and praised its curriculum. I didn't have the time or money to attend, but here was my chance. I've always felt that when you stop learning, they shovel the dirt over you.

Naimoli swings for the fences

Former Anchor Glass CEO now aims for major leagues.

By CHRIS ROUSH
Tribune Staff Writer

TAMPA — More than 30 years ago, bad grades forced Vincent J. Naimoli to trade in his football cleats for books at Notre Dame.

Now, if he is successful, Tampa businessman Naimoli will need to be fitted for some new shoes: the metal spikes worn by baseball players.

Naimoli is the managing general partner of a group that announced last week it has reached an agreement to purchase the San Francisco Giants for $111 million and move them to St. Petersburg's Suncoast Dome.

In that position, he's placed the psyche of the entire Tampa Bay area, which desperately wants to be known as a major league area, on his shoulders.

But just who is Vince Naimoli and where did he get the money to help buy a baseball team?

Naimoli was not in the dome for last week's announcement and so far has escaped the public's eye. St. Petersburg Assistant City Manager Rick Dodge said Friday that Naimoli was traveling on business involved in the deal to buy the Giants. He's expected to return Friday and discuss the deal and its plans.

Naimoli's secretary, who had spent most of Monday answering calls, said his Tampa office would not field any questions until then.

But business analysts and associates describe him as a hands-on, aggressive businessman who looks people in the eye when he talks and, like a football coach, demands 110 percent from his team. A slight stutterer, Naimoli is a bear of a man who made his money leading the reorganization of a Fortune 500 company.

"He's a terrific guy and a great businessman," said Jack Critchfield, chairman of the board and chief executive officer of Florida Progress Corp., the parent of Florida Power, who spearheaded the effort to bring the Giants to St. Petersburg.

"I think we can be very grateful that he's been willing to be involved in a major way in the ownership group," Critchfield added Monday afternoon.

"I think the world of him," says Richard Lilly, director of research with J.W. Charles Securities in Boca Raton, who followed Naimoli's Anchor Glass when it was a publicly traded company. "He's a fabulous individual. The Tampa Bay area needs more people like him."

Naimoli had been president, chairman and chief executive of the company, helping organize a leveraged buyout of the glass division of Anchor Hocking Corp.

1989 when a Mexican company, Vitro S.A., bought out Tampa-based Anchor Glass Container Corp. after it suffered heavy financial losses. It was a bitter battle, and Naimoli left the company for other business interests.

His life has been one of hurdles and successes.

Raised in Patterson, N.J., the 54-year-old Naimoli won a Navy ROTC scholarship to attend the University of Notre Dame. He tried to walk on to the football team, but a poor performance in the classroom forced him to abandon that idea.

Two years ago, Naimoli, who graduated from Notre Dame in 1959, returned triumphantly to the Fighting Irish football field as one of the alumni chosen to be a head coach in the team's annual Blue and Gold Game.

His business career took off in the can and beverage industry. Naimoli is a former vice president of Alleghany Beverage Corp. in Baltimore and a former vice president of

Tribune file photograph

Vincent J. Naimoli, former CEO of Anchor Glass, is now managing general partner of the group trying to bring the Giants to the bay area.

Vincent J. Naimoli

■ **Position:** Managing general partner of group that has signed agreement to buy San Francisco Giants and move them to St. Petersburg's Suncoast Dome.

■ **Age:** 54

■ **Business interests:** Chairman, president and chief executive officer of Anchor Industries International Inc., an operating and holding company he formed after leaving Anchor Glass in late 1989. Is also chairman and CEO of Doehler-Jarvis Corp. of Toledo, Ohio, an automotive parts supplier. Naimoli also sits on the boards of Florida Progress Corp. and Lincoln Foodservice Products Inc., a Fort Wayne, Ind., manufacturer of aluminum cooking equipment.

■ **Education:** Graduate in engineering.

Tampa Tribune, 1985
Reprinted with permission of The Tampa Tribune

ERNST & YOUNG LLP

Inc.

Merrill L

KNIGHT

1995 FLORIDA
ENTREPRENEUR OF THE YEAR

I got lots of compliments at CCC, but not much pay. One day during a presentation to Bob Hatfield, the company's CEO, I said, "I bet I can turn our market share in food around." And I did. "Congratulations, you did it," CCC's president told me. "How about a raise?" I countered, knowing that I was making a third of what my predecessor in the food division made.

"Be patient," was the response. But telling me to be patient is like telling a baby not to cry. Besides, I had a family to feed and had accomplished what others had failed to do.

Then, life took an unexpected turn. I was working on a deal with Allegheny Beverage Corp., the second-largest Pepsi franchise holder, trying to get back the business CCC had lost. Apparently, I had impressed the chairman, and although he had no intention of giving us back the account, he offered me a job.

No, thanks, I told him. But he was persistent and finally the lure of being the president of a stock exchange-listed company was too tempting to resist. Not only was it a great job, my salary tripled and I got a Mercedes as a company car.

Vince, with staff member, Congressman Bill Young, Vince's wife, Lenda and her sister, Glenda

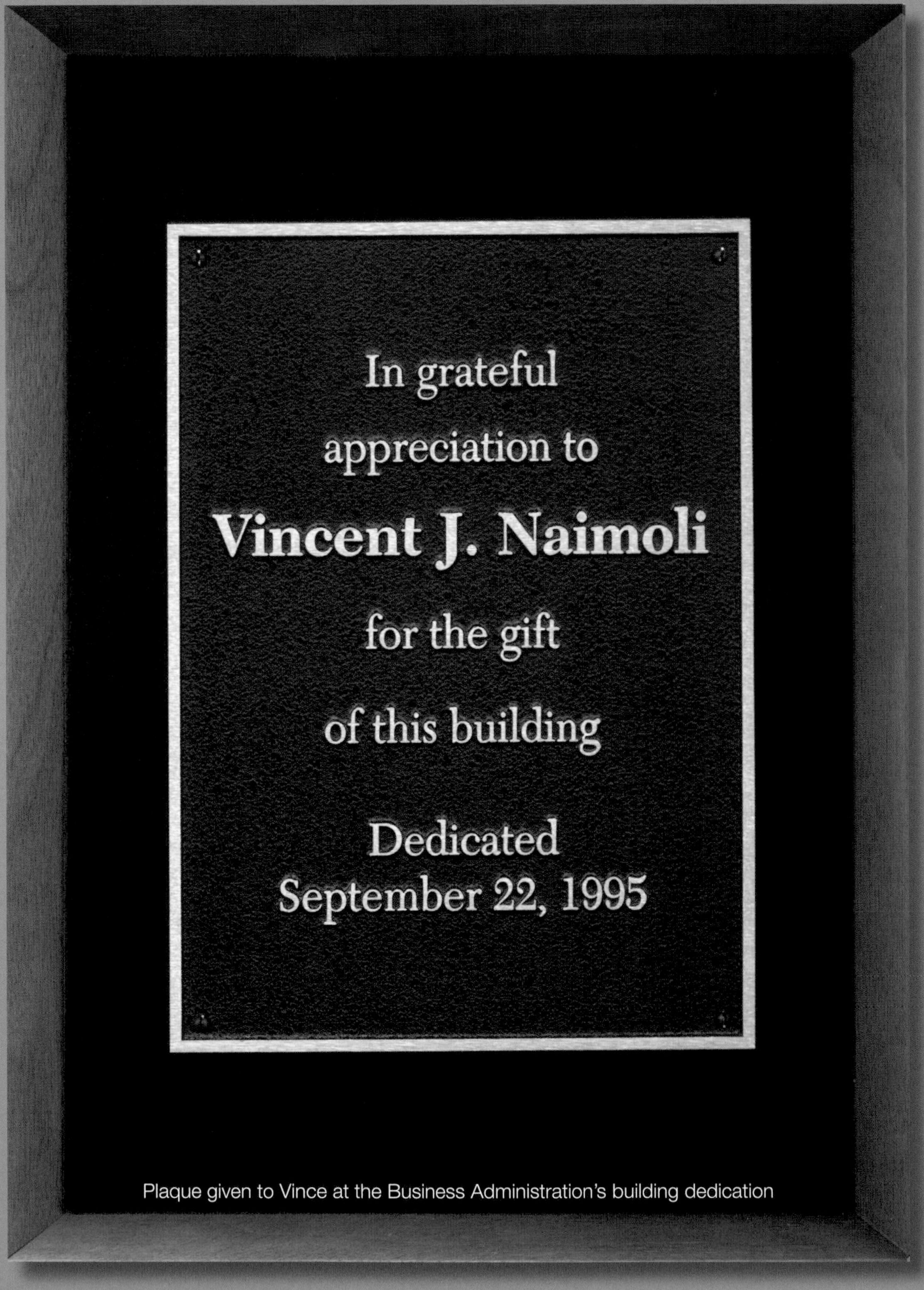

In grateful
appreciation to

Vincent J. Naimoli

for the gift

of this building

Dedicated
September 22, 1995

Plaque given to Vince at the Business Administration's building dedication

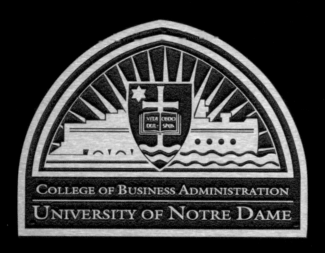

COLLEGE OF BUSINESS ADMINISTRATION

UNIVERSITY OF NOTRE DAME

Forbes magazine, 1985

The challenges started right away. Pepsi wanted to take the franchise away because we weren't using an approved ingredient in the beverage. I tried to reason with Pepsi. "If you don't take any action, I promise it won't happen again and I'll make our plants No. 1 in quality in all of Pepsi," I told Mr. Bonomo, the president of Pepsi. I gathered the troops together and pleaded for their help. They knew exactly what to do. I was able to make the company No. 1 in quality in Pepsi-Cola and increase our market share over Coca-Cola, but after six months, I realized that the chairman and I didn't see eye-to-eye and that this job wasn't right for me.

So, when world-renowned head hunter Gardner Heidrick, founder of Heidrick & Struggles, called in 1977 to tell me he had a job I would love,

I was intrigued. Turns out the job was senior vice president at the Tampa-based Jim Walter Corp. which had 42 divisions, including coke, iron and chemicals, pipe, coal and building products.

Goodbye frigid winters, hello sunny Florida. I packed my bags, along with a little trepidation, which dissipated when I realized how nice Tampa is.

I greatly admired Jim Walter, who was very smart, business savvy and a wonderful person. But it seemed like Jim was never going to retire, which meant that President Joe Cordell wouldn't take his place, which meant that I wouldn't be president. At least not anytime soon.

So about four years later, when a head hunter asked me to work for Anchor Hocking, I decided it was the right move. The glass industry was shattering (pardon the pun) and I wanted to do something to repair it. I was in charge of three divisions but decided to focus on the glass container division. The way to save it, I thought, was to buy it out and start over. I spent March 1983 putting together a deal. It was a $75 million dollar deal. I knew how to operate things, but didn't know how to borrow money. That didn't stop me.

I was on a plane to New York City to meet with Marty Segal, a Kidder Peabody investment banker, who was locating a leveraged buyout firm to help me borrow the money, when I came across an article in *Business Week* about Wesray, one of the first leveraged buyout firms.

I met with three big-name leveraged buyout firms, but I was intrigued with

Wesray's reputation so I set up a meeting. I was so impressed with Ray Chambers and Bill Simon, a former Secretary of the Treasury, that I decided to do the deal with them. To my amazement, it was done in three weeks.

When it was time to gather the Anchor Hocking glass container division plant and sales managers, I knew the rumors would be flying. I wanted to make sure I was the one dispensing the facts, so I had to disrupt their holiday weekend. They were to meet me Easter Sunday at the Lancaster, Ohio Country Club. Most of these employees had worked at Anchor their whole career and they were leery.

When I arrived, 35 sets of anxious eyes scrutinized me as they waited to hear what the news was and how it would affect them.

"I have good news and bad news," I told them. "The good news is that we are going to spin off from Anchor Hocking. You will all be owners and get stock. The bad news is that the stock is worthless. It will be worth something if we all work hard and make it worth something."

The reality was grim. The once-thriving division, which became Anchor Glass Container Corp., was losing $1 million a year. "We can't match our biggest competitor in numbers but if we outwork them, we can beat them," I told the members of the company's most recalcitrant union. "I have a job because you have a job. If you do your job, I'll have a job. If not, neither of us will have jobs."

I had just as much to lose, perhaps even more, because I put all the money I had into the venture. But the staff didn't know that.

Collage given to Vince when leaving Continental Can Corporation

They knew we were serious because I and the staff visited every one of our 30 plants monthly. But I had a handle on the situation and felt better knowing that Jim Walter, who I trusted and admired, was a board member.

I moved Anchor Glass Container Corp. from Lancaster, Ohio, to Tampa. I couldn't afford to give anyone a raise but since they wouldn't have to pay state income tax in Florida as they did in Ohio, they would have more money in their paychecks.

The Tampa headquarters were in a brand-new building on Cypress Street. The moving vans were packed, the employees were on their way. It was Labor Day weekend and I was in Washington, D.C., but my trip was interrupted with an urgent phone call. "There's a problem regarding the readiness of the building," I was told. I thought about the problem and figured out a solution. So on Tuesday morning at 10 a.m., the predicament was resolved and we were able to move in.

Florida Trend, 1992

TO THE RESCUE

Hard Times? Call Naimoli

If every troubled company could tap into **Vince Naimoli's** management skills, it's a good bet we'd see far fewer bankruptcy filings.

Naimoli, 54, former chairman and CEO of Tampa-based Anchor Glass Corp., doesn't need the cash – he took home $20 million when Mexico's Vitro S.A. acquired Anchor in 1989. But he likes the challenge and satisfaction of putting companies back on track.

In 1990, Naimoli tackled Georgia-based Electrolux Corp. In nine months, he cut costs, increased sales and implemented a financial restructuring. By the end of the year, Naimoli says, "I was able to re-place myself with a permanent chairman."

About a year ago, Naimoli took the helm of Toledo, Ohio-based Doehler-Jarvis Inc., a producer of aluminum die castings. Naimoli remains based in Tampa and runs the company as what he calls "a part-time CEO." It, too, "was rescued," Naimoli says. Just another day at the office.

In addition to his duties at Doehler-Jarvis, Naimoli is involved in a dizzying array of other projects. In early 1991, he joined forces with Wesray Capital, one of the early LBO firms. Working with Wesray, Naimoli set up Lancaster Capital, a mergers-and-acquisition fund. When Naimoli is not teaming with Wesray, he works through his own firm, Anchor Industries. Right now he is bidding on three acquisitions – all industrial product companies he won't name.

Vince Naimoli has made the turnaround his playground.

About 120 people moved to Tampa. They were from a small town so the Sunshine State was a strange land to them. Since they didn't know anyone in their new town, I hosted monthly barbecues so they could have a social life.

My social life was on the upswing, too, since I'd met my future wife, Lenda, a vivacious Eastern Airlines flight attendant, on a business trip. I was hard at work every time she passed my seat. "Stop working and have some fun," she urged me. I didn't stop working, at least right then, but I decided to set aside some time that night to take her out.

"How about going out for a drink?" I asked her as I left the plane. But she was reluctant and embarrassed because I asked her in front of the captain and crew. "He really wasn't my type and besides I wasn't looking for a relationship," Lenda recalled. "But he was very, very persistent so I told him where I was staying."

I wined and dined her but that didn't impress her much. "But then he took me to church. He was the only man who ever took me to church. That was it for me. We still go to church on Sundays," Lenda said.

Talk about a match made in heaven, or at least at 35,000 feet! We fell in love and were married on Oct. 12, 1981, about nine months after we met.

Being the wife of Vince Naimoli has its perks, but Lenda is her own person and wants to keep it that way. On one flight, as she was handing out *Business Week*, which contained a feature article about me, a passenger realized she was my wife and asked her why she was still working. Never at a loss for words, she had a quick reply: "I love my husband, I love my job and I love my identity."

Lenda had a few surprises for me, too, She has an identical twin, Glenda. They still dress alike, right down to their earrings. Both retired Eastern airline stewardesses, they were known as "the flying saucy twins" and were also crowned Miss AM and Miss FM at a radio station in Winston Salem, N.C. during their teen years. Ironically, we just met the new owner of the radio station. "I often wondered who those girls were in that picture in my desk," he said.

The two have been known to use their indistinguishable faces to their advantage. When one twin could pass the driving test, but the other wasn't sure she could, what else could they do? Thanks to Lenda, Glenda got her license when she was 16 in Welcome, N.C., their home town. Lenda was so convincing that when she went the next day to get her own license and was assigned to the same tester, she passed with flying colors. No one ever discovered their plot.

The two decided not to test their luck when Glenda moved to Florida 22 years ago and needed to get a new license. Now, Glenda lives about 20 minutes from us and since she plays tennis or golf every day at Tampa Palms Country Club, Lenda kids her about being "Miss Tampa Palms."

The sisters still talk about the "trading places" caper that backfired. Lenda took a flight assignment for Glenda; they figured as long as one of them showed up there wasn't a problem. But Lenda's supervisor was suspicious and called her on the carpet. When she discovered the truth, she told her they would both be fired if it happened again. That was the end of those switches.

Shortly after Glenda married Ed Young, he was sent to Vietnam, where he was Gen. Westmoreland's briefing advisor. Glenda missed Ed terribly and since she and Lenda had round-the-world Eastern Airlines passes, off they went. But they couldn't get into Saigon. Undaunted, they found an Air Force man to contact Ed. He explained the quandary to Gen. Westmoreland, who had a plan. "I'll approve bringing them in as entertainers," the general said.

They didn't have to sing or dance and they saw the shells from the gunfire bursting from their perch atop the Rex Hotel. I'm still flabbergasted that they were able to pull that off and often tease them about being Vietnam vets. (Ed, a 28-year-Navy veteran who retired as a captain, recently passed away).

When Lenda decided she wanted to have a family, she had her own way of telling me. She often leaves me notes, so I wasn't surprised to find one under my pillow one day. "I'm ready to start a family," she wrote. Our daughter, Lindsey, another Notre Dame grad, was born in 1983. She adores animals, just like her Mom, and has the kindest heart. She lives in California, where she is pursuing her veterinary doctorate degree (which she will receive in 2011). She's across the country, but we hear from her frequently. She has called us every day since she moved away.

When Lindsey was a toddler, my corporate life reached a pinnacle. Anchor Glass was going to be listed on the stock exchange; the company was going public. This was an immense opportunity and word spread like wildfire. Eighty percent of the 10,000 or so employees bought stock in the company.

I was the role model for hard work. Not much could stop me, except when I thought I was having a heart attack while doing a European version of the "road show" to sell the Anchor stock to investors in Zurich. I went to a German doctor, and even though we couldn't communicate well, I did learn that I wasn't having a heart attack.

I was relieved, but in horrific pain and couldn't wait to get home. As I

L-R: Vince's father Ralph; mother Margaret; Rev. Hesburg, C.S.C.; Lenda and Vince

boarded the Concorde, I was sweating profusely and bent over in pain. What could be worse? I thought. I looked at the passenger in the seat across from me. It was Billie Jean King, whom I admire tremendously. But there was no way I could talk to her. Not only was I in severe pain, I was embarrassed that I was sweating from every single pore.

The pain persisted when we got home. "I feel terrible," I told Lenda, who took me to a walk-in clinic on a Saturday. The doctor told me that I had pericarditis, a swelling and irritation of the sac surrounding the heart. It's not something that usually causes repercussions if you take care of it, but the relentless pain lasts for hours, even days and doesn't diminish even when you rest.

"You are really sick and need to be in the hospital," the doctor said. I spent a grueling week in intensive care. When I got out, there was no time to waste and despite still feeling ill, I had to start the "road show" for American investors.

A few years later, Lenda retired after 24 years with Eastern Airlines. When she left, she got lifetime passes to fly, which sounded like the ultimate perk. "I didn't know Eastern was going to die before I did," she quipped.

Little did I know there were more changes ahead. In 1989, I received an unsolicited offer to sell Anchor. The company had come so far. The employees all worked hard and at the end of the first year we had a million dollar profit. And when we sold it, Wesray, which had put in $1 million to help buy Anchor Glass, made $240 million. The key managers made more than a million dollars each and everyone who bought stock in the company when we listed it at least doubled their investment.

The company was named the third most profitable in the world in the Forbes 500. I was so elated to be CEO that it didn't even bother me when I got a letter from a consultant telling me I was the most underpaid CEO of any company. In fact, I tossed the letter, although now I think I should have saved it.

Raymond Hollaway, the former vice president and general manager of Anchor Hocking's closure division and an excellent golfer, remembers those days. "When they purchased Anchor Glass Container Corporation it was deeply in debt. By 1987, Vince turned the firm into the nation's third most profitable company, and when he sold Anchor Glass, sales were soaring past $1 billion," he recalled.

"He was my boss on paper but he always treated me as an equal and never tried to micromanage my division. My division always had his full support. When results were good he gave all the credit to division management. When they were not, he shouldered part of the responsibility. He was one of four mentors that helped shape my 34-year career there."

I thought I left Anchor in capable hands and that the employees were taken care of. That wasn't the case. We sold Anchor to Vitro, a very fine company. Vitro, which had an excellent CEO, put an outstanding president in charge of its new subsidiary, Anchor Glass. But about a year later, the president, who was a Mormon, had a calling and left for a mission. This was followed by more bad news. Vitro's CEO left to take a succession of jobs, including Minister of Energy for Mexico.

Anchor Glass president's successor made some really questionable business deals and the company suffered. The glass container division, my pride and joy, went bankrupt. It was purchased, but the next thing I heard, the pension fund was under-funded. When we sold it, the pension fund was over-funded and we considered doing a reversion to free up the excess cash. But we never did.

I wanted to get to the bottom of it and went to a Pension Board Guarantee Corporation (PBGC) meeting where it was being discussed. There, I ran into one of my former Anchor colleagues who was very distressed. "I am supposed to be getting $1,500 a month pension and I'm getting $750. I can't live on it and I can't afford to hire a lawyer. Can you do anything?"

I hired a lawyer and filed a class action suit and won. Everyone got what they were entitled to, but the PBGC refused to join the lawsuit or go after the guy who was responsible.

Every employee got their full pension, but the PBGC, a government agency funded by taxpayers, was out the $80 million it cost to put things right. About six months ago, the PBGC announced its deficit was down to $13 billion… only $13 billion… I was astounded that it would consider that a feather in its cap. I wrote PBGC a terse letter telling them that it would have been down another $80 million if they had gone after the person responsible for the Anchor debacle.

Meanwhile, I had a good deal of money, but didn't really have a worthwhile business pursuit. And as everyone knows, I love to work, so I created Anchor Industries International, a holding investment company.

I had barely settled in when my pal Ray Chambers called, asking for help with Wesray's 22 companies. I was brought on as the president of the management company called Harding Resources and my first order of business was to sell 21 of the companies. The remaining one, Electrolux, which manufactured high-quality cleaning machines, needed some TLC. After a weeklong audit of the company, I knew the problem. The CEO wasn't the best person for the job. I delivered the news to Ray, thinking I'd done my job and would be on my way.

"OK, then I want you to be the interim CEO," he told me. No way, I thought. "I never asked for that. I'm not sure I want to do that," I told him. Somehow, he and Wells Fargo, the Electrolux lead bank (which had also been Anchor Glass' lead bank) persuaded me to try it for a year. The year whizzed by, and I turned the company around.

Taking down-and-out companies and turning them around was so invigorating I couldn't wait for my next challenge.

It came in the form of Doehler-Jarvis Inc., which manufactured precision automotive/truck components and was owned by Banker's Trust, Loeb Partners and Farley Industries. The company, which supplied 60 percent of transmission cases for Ford, was in desperate shape and preparing to file for bankruptcy. We really needed a price increase from Ford. "If we don't get the price increase, we'll have to file for bankruptcy and your supply will be interrupted," I somberly and respectfully told the Ford purchasing execs.

Waiting for their answer was gut-wrenching. I had never filed for bankruptcy and couldn't stand the thought. For me, that would have been the ultimate failure. Finally, on Christmas Eve, I got a call. "You've got the price increase," I was told. Ah, what a holiday that was.

People ask how I turned these companies around. Here are two secrets. All had one thing in common: too much fat. If you skim the fat, much like you would do to a pot of chicken soup, you will have a healthier product. Also, I learned that if you listen to the lowest paid person, the person on the front line, you'll find out the problems as well as the solutions.

Challenges were lining up like birds on a wire. Next was my appointment to the board of Harvard Industries, an auto parts company, a month after it emerged from bankruptcy reorganization. After about six months, I became CEO and the company attained almost $7 million in earnings — up from a loss of $131 million under the former CEO a year earlier.

The cash registers were still jangling when ING asked me to join the board of Ladish, which manufactures high-tech magnesium aerospace, aircraft and nuclear parts. The company, which had just gotten out of bankruptcy, had lost the illustrious Pratt -Whitney account. Ladish's CEO didn't want the board and others to know, but the word got out and he was fired. I was asked by ING to step in and take over the mess.

I knew we needed another high-profile client, so I scheduled a meeting with General Electric. They drove a hard bargain, but ultimately had a proposal for me. "Let us come in and show you how we could cut costs 35 percent," they countered. "Sure," I told them, although I had my doubts about how they would cut 35 percent. But they streamlined the operations and it worked.

I was at the top of my game and couldn't have been happier. I was CEO simultaneously of Harvard Industries, Doehler-Jarvis and Ladish Corp., all Fortune 500 companies. And I was voted Florida Entrepreneur of the Year in the "turnaround" category in 1995. What a life! While Ladish was still thriving and had adequate cash flow, the new CEO of Harvard Industries and Doehler-Jarvis decided to take them into bankruptcy.

Although the pay was great, the rewards awesome, life threw me a curveball. I was recruited in 1991 to bring baseball to Tampa Bay. I knew that would be a 24/7 job, so I had to give up all my money-making pursuits and get ready to batter up.

The Baseball Years

Vince celebrates on the front page of the Tampa Tribune

The dream of owning a baseball team

THE WORD WAS OUT: ST. PETERSBURG WAS FINALLY GETTING A BASEBALL TEAM. WHEN THE PHONE JANGLED THAT DAY IN 1995, I FIGURED IT WAS THE INTREPID *TAMPA TRIBUNE* SPORTS EDITOR TOM MCEWEN. "CONGRATULATIONS," HE UTTERED. "BUT GET READY. YOUR LIFE IS NEVER GOING TO BE THE SAME. YOU'D BETTER BE VERY THICK-SKINNED."

I was befuddled. What was he talking about? Geez, did the press always have to be so cynical? Was this one of McEwen's offbeat jokes or an ominous warning I should take seriously?

Vince at a baseball game

Turns out all the alligator hides in the Everglades wouldn't be enough to protect me from the backlash I'd encounter. But who knew? I was spending all of my energy and a lot of my money to lure a team to Tampa Bay at great sacrifice to my earning power, figuring it would improve the social and economic conditions in the area.

Local leaders had made several attempts to draw a Major League Baseball team, including the Chicago White Sox, Minnesota Twins and Texas Rangers; they all failed. Sports fans were left to wonder which would come first: a home team or the turn of the century. I shared those doubts but hoped someday I'd be cheering from the sidelines when the first pitch was thrown. I didn't dream that fate would rest on my shoulders.

The inspiration came, like many do, during a leisurely meal with a Notre Dame friend in 1989. Andy McKenna and I were eating breakfast, talking sports and catching up. And then came the million-dollar question.

"Why don't you get a baseball team for Tampa Bay? It's the biggest thing you could do for the community, economic impact wise," he said. McKenna, who was then chairman of the board of trustees at Notre Dame, chairman of the Chicago Cubs and a very respected Chicago businessman, had saved the White Sox for Chicago in the early '80s, so he knew how to play the game. But still…

"We have a group trying to get a team and I don't want to be an interloper," I replied. Besides, life was good and for once I was enjoying the status quo, having just sold Anchor Glass Container at a substantial profit. There was no need to turn my life upside down.

Vince and Ted Williams at a baseball game

But, two years later, when Major League Baseball snubbed St. Petersburg and chose South Florida and Denver for expansion teams, I thought: Enough, it's time to step up to the plate.

I didn't realize that convincing the Major League Baseball ownership committee to bring a team to Tampa Bay would be more frustrating than trying to patch a tire with Scotch tape. Despite my glowing reports about the area, I couldn't change the perception that St. Petersburg was a "time-out spot," a place to send sports teams that did not conform. "We'll move you to St. Pete," owners would threaten certain teams. And since the city had an empty stadium, it became a pawn.

That wasn't the way I saw it. We had an empty stadium, a bustling city, welcoming sports fans and perfect weather. What's not to like?

I wasn't going to give up. Courage and determination are as much a part of my being as my skin and bones. I figured those traits, along with my willpower and problem-solving skills, would compensate for being a neophyte at baseball team acquisition. I always admired McDonald's founder Ray Kroc's tenacity and perseverance which propelled him to success. I'd been called tenacious and considered it a compliment. Besides, I'd acquired many companies, this couldn't be that much different, right?

Wrong. I spent most of my time on the phone, trying to convince MLB executives that Tampa Bay was a great place for a team. Ten thousand (or more) phone calls, ten thousand frustrations.

Some claim I was thin-skinned (they were right about that), cheap (wrong) and tough-hearted (wrong again). But somewhere along the way, I wish I had been given credit for my doggedness and other admirable traits.

Although I knew buying a team wouldn't be simple, I never imagined it would be so arduous. I would have been really disheartened without the support I received. City Administrator Rick Dodge's daily pep talks kept my spirits up. He was riding the baseball commissioner, as were U.S. Sen. Connie Mack and others. I was also grateful for the unwavering support of Dr. Jack Critchfield who was the CEO of

Florida Progress Corp.

In June 1991, I serendipitously stepped into the tumultuous world of baseball ownership. It was like a plunge into an ice-cold pool. There's no use putting in one toe at a time. It's better to just dive in and acclimate quickly.

My foray began at Morgan Stanley. "Would you be interested in the Mariners?" they asked. "Our partnership has a third of the equity and we loaned the managing partner his two thirds, but his stock, which is the collateral for the loan, is in the tank."

I had a question of my own: "What if I bought his two-thirds without the accrued interest and I move the team to

Vince and Paul Mainieri,
then baseball coach at Notre Dame

St. Pete because we have a facility?" They liked the idea, but then reality struck me: I made a deal to buy this loan but I needed someone with baseball expertise to guide me. I called Gene Fanning, a Notre Dame alum and an investor in the White Sox, and Andy McKenna.

Vince, rebuilding what is now, Tropicana Field

They introduced me to Jerry Reinsdorf, the principal owner and managing partner of the Chicago White Sox and a very influential member of the baseball ownership committee, who told me that a meeting was imminent between the Mariners and a group of Japanese investors. "We're going to tell them that they can put up the money for the team but they can't have operating control. I don't think they'll go for that, so call me," Jerry said. Jerry, like me, is a former Brooklyn Dodger fan and I admire his business acumen very much.

That night, different scenarios raced through my mind. All of them had one thing in common: This was going to be a great adventure. I was pumped and ready to make a deal. So, I wasn't prepared for the news I got the next morning.

"You won't believe this, but the Japanese agreed to everything," Jerry said incredulously.

I figured it was over. I was ready to give up, but others, including the mayor of St. Petersburg, weren't going to let me. "Hey," the mayor told me in mid-1991. "The San Francisco Giants are for sale. Will you put together a group and manage a buyout?"

No way, I thought. "I'm not interested. I'm busy with other things," I told him. But after three weeks of constant coaxing,

I threw up my hands and gave in.

This deal looked much more promising than the last one. I was leading a group of investors with a $115 million signed contract to buy the Giants from Bob Lurie, who owned the team, and whisk them to the Sunshine State.

"I'm going to go around and see all the owners in baseball. I'm not sure whether the vote is going to be 28-0 or 27-1 to make the transfer, but we're gonna get it done," Lurie assured me.

I was on top of the world. The night before I was leaving for Phoenix to seal the deal, the phone rang. It was Lurie, and he was frantic. "You better get here right away," he said, his voice quivering. "We have a problem."

My euphoria evaporated like a spring shower. Turns out, the majority had gone against him. Something had obviously gone down behind the scenes and I was beginning to feel like a star-crossed suitor.

Later, I found out that National Baseball

United States Marine Drum and Bugle Corps. entertain at the Inaugaural game, Tropicana Field, 1998

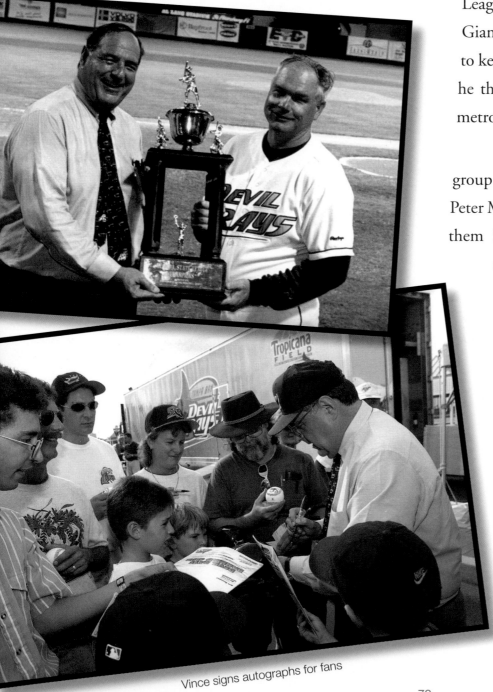

Vince accepts the Florida State League Championship Award, with Bill Evers, Manager, 1995

Vince signs autographs for fans

League President Bill White, a former Giants player, had campaigned heavily to keep the team in California because he thought it should play in a major metropolitan area like San Francisco.

The Giants were sold to a group headed by former Giants director Peter Magowan which promised to keep them in California. They paid $100 million for the team, which was $10 million less than we offered, but the old proverb of location, location, location sealed the deal for them. In retrospect, Peter did a great job with the team and became a fine friend. He was able to get a beautiful new stadium in downtown San Francisco to replace outmoded Candlestick Park. That $10 million provided fodder for Notre

Dame Coach Lou Holtz's speeches. Whenever I'm in the audience, he makes sure to point me out as the worst salesman in the world.

Now, it's almost funny, but at the time, I was really galled. We had a signed contract and were offering $10 million more and they passed on our offer. Frustrated and dejected, I threw up my hands in defeat.

This was supposed to be an ironclad deal and St. Petersburg was not about to let it go without a fight, so the city sued the city of San Francisco for $3 billion, for the loss of economic benefit. Rick Dodge, St. Pete's City Administrator, was quoted as saying, "The

Vince enjoying a game

community had rights they wanted protected and we're going to protect them. I think about what Al Capone said: 'You can get a lot of cooperation with a smile and you get a lot more cooperation with a smile and a gun.' The gun here is righteousness. We did things right, the business way that's correct and baseball should have recognized that and acted appropriately."

My group and I were not a part of the lawsuit and didn't want to be. I was afraid we would alienate the owners and we'd never get a team. But we watched and waited, quietly rooting for St. Petersburg.

Vince surveys the crowd at Tropicana Field

San Francisco fought back. There were a lot of tightly knotted stomachs. Just when we felt like we were at the bottom of the ninth with two outs, we got a winning play. The city didn't get any money, but we were quietly confident we'd get an expansion team. That was the impetus the city needed to drop the lawsuit.

At the time, I thought the botched deal was one of bleakest moments of my life, but now I realize it was fortuitous that it tanked. The stadium needed a lot of work and there wouldn't have been time for the renovations. Now, we had a chance to transform the stadium and start with a new team, to make a name for ourselves with our own brand.

They say good things happen to those who wait. Maybe that's true, but I can't say I waited patiently. At one point, the contract almost fell through. We were told we could get the team for $115 million, plus the forgiveness of $25 million in TV revenues. A good deal, I thought as I shared celebratory drinks with the press at The Breakers in Palm Beach, where the transaction was to be announced in March 1995. But the celebration was cut short when I listened to a terse voice mail from Jerry Colangelo,

Vince and Lenda with Bishop Lynch

the managing partner of the Arizona Diamondbacks, the other team to be awarded a franchise in the morning.

"I have good and bad news," he told me. "The good news is that we're definitely getting the franchise. I'll tell you the bad news in the morning." It was 1 a.m. so I couldn't call him back so I tossed and turned all night, imagining the worst. The news was bad; the price had been jacked up to $130 million, plus the forgiveness of $25 million in TV revenues. "I'm outta here," I told him.

"Wait a minute, I have an idea," my brother Ray said. His plan to change the timing of when the money was due saved the deal (in economic terms it's called present value).

I still found it hard to believe

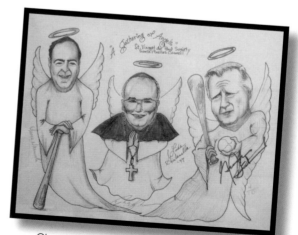
Charactiture of Vince, Bishop Lynch and George Steinbrener

that it was a done deal. So even though the vote was 28-0 to make the Tampa Bay Devil Rays and the Arizona Diamondbacks the 29th and 30th expansion teams in Major League Baseball, I was a bundle of emotions. Finally, I relaxed, let out a gargantuan sigh, then realized there was no time for a prolonged celebration. We had a lot of work to do. It was 1995; we weren't scheduled to play until 1998, but we were nowhere near ready for that first pitch.

Vince with Tom Foley (left), third base coach, Hal McRae, second manager
and two minor league players

Tampa Bay Devil Rays Inaugural Team, 1998

Tampa Bay Devil Rays open season in Japan
vs the New York Yankees, 2004

In April, St. Petersburg and the Rays signed a 30-year lease for the team to play all home games beginning in 1998 at the Thunderdome (later renamed Tropicana Field). And then… our first player, 6'4" right-handed pitcher Adam Sisk, put pen to paper. We were on our way! Things seemed to really fall in place when 24 minor-league free agents assembled for the first mini-camp in June 1995.

The Rays were voted into the American League in 1997, the same year we signed superstar third baseman and Hall of Famer Wade Boggs, who would make us famous two years later when he tallied his 3,000th career hit on a home run, the only Rays player so far to reach that mark. We also signed Fred McGriff, a Tampa native and five time All-Star who was the Rays' opening day starter at first base for the first four seasons. In my opinion, he should have a spot in the Major League Baseball Hall of Fame.

The euphoria was building to a crescendo; I felt like Leonard Bernstein conducting Tchaikovsky's Fifth Symphony. My baton was poised, but could I execute the perfect pitch, the right tempo? Was it possible to instill the emotional intensity and loyalty and acquire all the talent we needed to pull this off?

I got my answer Dec. 6, 1997 when the first tickets went on sale: Opening Day sold out in 17 minutes. Seventeen minutes! You can't even find a place to park at a stadium in 17 minutes. I walked along the long line of people waiting to buy tickets, shaking hands and thanking everyone. I even bought them coffee and doughnuts.

And when I saw 45,000 buoyant fans at the first game in March 1998, I forgot the years of aggravation. Hall of Famers Ted Williams, Stan Musial, Al Lopez and Monte Irvin threw out the ceremonial first pitches on that glorious spring day. It was like welcoming a new baby into the family, being cocooned in a warm, loving embrace. The evening before our inaugural game, we had a black-tie gala for the investors and sponsors with the U.S. Marine Drum and Bugle Corps providing the entertainment.

As the gates opened the next day, I felt a swell of pride as the team manager, some of the players and I greeted the crowd who entered the rotunda, shaking hands and thanking everyone. The team president and manager and certain players continue this practice today and I'm very proud. "Our fans are our customers. Without our customers, we don't have a business. I can assure you, we want to love you as much as you want to love us," I told the cheering fans.

The feel-good mood didn't last long. The team lost to the Detroit Tigers 11-6, despite Boggs' two-run homer. The fans were somber. It was as if 45,000 shoulders slumped simultaneously. It was not the start I envisioned, but I knew we had to keep the faith, that we'd make a comeback. And I was right. The next day was April Fool's Day, but the joke was on

Tampa Bay Rays play game against the Notre Dame baseball team

Team players are introduced at Inaugural game, 1998

the Detroit Tigers as the Devil Rays won, 11-8. "Say hello to victory, Tampa Bay!" radio commentator Paul Olden boomed.

In baseball, when you win, it's supreme elation. When you lose it's supreme depression. We won and it sure felt good. But I knew the feeling would only last until our next loss. The baseball world is like Busch Gardens' roller coaster SheiKra, full of gut-wrenching twists and turns with an electrifying 70 mph drop. I thought the fans would hang on for dear life and enjoy the ride.

I found out otherwise. After we lost the first game, only 29,000 turned out for the second game. I thought we would have sold out the whole opening season or at least the opening series and I was disappointed that there weren't more people to witness the team's first win.

Here's the truth: fans are fickle. "People buy a $5 ticket and they think they own you," ex-Tampa Mayor Dick Grecco had warned me.

When we lost, I'd sleep fitfully, waking up and replaying everything in my mind. In the replays, we'd always win. Dream on, my mind kept telling me.

I went to virtually all the games and cheered. When I sat in the stands with the fans, I controlled my frustration when the team floundered. But when I sat in my suite or my office, I'd throw my hat down and mutter under my breath about the umpires' calls and other things.

I learned one steadfast rule: I never changed seats once the game started. One superstition in baseball is that if the team is behind, move your seat. If they are ahead, stay where you are. I come to believe that unofficial "rule" the hard way. In 2003, I was in Chicago watching the Rays play the White

Inaugural game at Tropicana Field

2006 World Baseball Classic, Inaugural Tournament

Sox, and the Rays were in the lead. I had two grandsons with me and it was cold and rainy. Jerry Reinsdorf kindly invited us to take shelter in a suite. Grateful to be out of the dreadful weather, we agreed. The Rays lost. The next night, the same thing happened. In the third game, I politely declined. The Rays won.

I was learning a lot about baseball. And not all of it was good. I had exchanged a high-paying career for a new life with no remuneration and a lot of frustration. I didn't want to regret it.

I'm tough and I don't back away from things. Grit and problem-solving skills took me from my humble start in Paterson, N.J., to Notre Dame, two master's degrees on scholarships, up the corporate ladder and then a career as a sought-after corporate turnaround specialist.

I'm a hard-hitter, but I think I'm good-hearted, kind of like Clint Eastwood's movie characters. And I'm a trusting soul, so when people give me their word and we shake on it, I figure it's good.

The "hit show" in 1999 showed me that was an illusion. The idea was to bring

Vince with Mickey Rooney and the Rays mascot

in veteran players to put on a show that would draw crowds. "You've got to build an image for the team, get some star players," I was told by one of our partners during a meeting with our vice president/general counsel, John Higgins.

"But what about the plan to develop slowly, to go through the draft?" I countered. "Who is going to pay for this?"

We'll put in the money, my partner assured me. He turned to the man next to him (also a partner), who agreed; he'd put in the money too. We signed five high-priced players, including Jose Canseco, Greg Vaughn and Vinny Castilla. We ran the payroll up close to $60 million, which made me sweat. My premonition of disaster came true. The hit show was a disaster, an expensive one. I felt scalded, as if someone had thrown a bucket of boiling water on me.

Jose Canseco had 31 home runs at the all-star break and was supposed to be in the all-star home run contest when catastrophe struck. He hurt his back and didn't play the second half of the season, which killed us. Critics said that the players were past their prime. They had a track record of being star players, but we didn't always see that. The fans were starting to grumble and abandon the team.

Meanwhile the payroll went up faster than the national debt and I was getting anxious. But that was nothing compared to the angst I felt when my partners reneged on their promise to help pay for the hit show. I couldn't believe someone would make a commitment and then renege.

So I anted up the money, about $30 million, to save the team. I didn't go

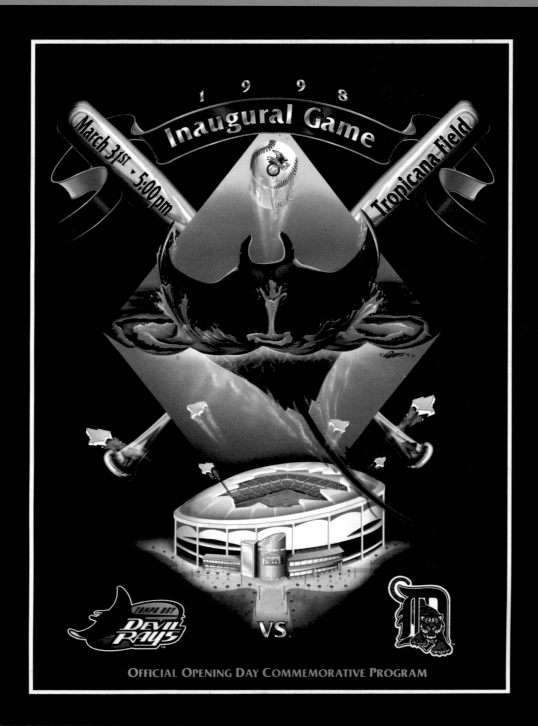

Illustration by Todd Dawes

Vince got three hits as he takes batting practice against Ronald McDonald

public with that tidbit (it was a private matter). If I had, it might have changed some perceptions about me. But if I hadn't put in the money, the team would have gone bankrupt.

I had great trepidation but I knew it had to be done. The team had to have a chance, so as my heart thumped, I took all the hard-earned money I had planned to use to buy another company someday and sunk it into the team. If I had been hooked up to an EKG machine, it probably would have registered a heartbeat erratic enough to warrant medical care.

This money was a rainy day fund. Who knew what emergencies would come up in the future? What if I didn't have the money to pay for them? On the other hand, the team needed me. In the end, I decided the rainy day had arrived. If things turned around, maybe I'd gaze upon a rainbow. I didn't dare hope for a pot of gold at the end of it, though.

It's a good thing I didn't, as we had given the players deferred payments so we were stuck with those bills till 2006.

Just when I was wondering if anything would ever go right again, some very good news arrived. I had been chosen for the prestigious Ellis Island Medal of Honor, given to those "who have been the very best that America has to offer." The list of other honorees reads like a Who's Who of influential, remarkable, inspirational people: astronauts, presidents, senators, judges...and me? I now had something in common with Ronald Reagan, Jimmy Carter, Hillary Clinton and John Glenn.

That was a tribute unlike any other, one I really appreciated. And thanks to George Steinbrenner for nominating me.

Baseball was still at the forefront of my mind, though. And it will always have a special place in my scrapbook of life. When I think about the baseball years, I laugh. And I cry. And I think it's time for my side of the story, to clear up a few falsehoods. I've been labeled cheap, called a tyrant and branded a loser. And there were backhanded compliments, too, like this one from an insensitive blogger, who like many, had no idea about the facts: "Yes, Vince Naimoli brought baseball to Tampa. What did he do with it after that? Nothing."

The stories about me were horrific. So I kept reading and listening, telling myself not to give up each time a headline shouted out a blatant lie or some know-nothing blogger stretched the truth. Perhaps there is some truth in the saying "never let facts stand the way of a good story."

Players pile on after winning the
2008 American League Championship

David Price, Commissioner, Bob Stewart and Vince,
first game of 2008 World Series

One of the more outlandish stories portrayed me as a screaming maniac who became incensed when a Mets scout "made a seemingly innocent mistake of using the private bathroom" in my suite before an April 2005 game.

Here's what really happened: When I walked into the general manager's suite, I saw a guy rummaging through my desk just prior to the amateur draft. He wasn't wearing the required ID badge, which to me was a dead giveaway that he was trespassing. There was also a huge No Admittance sign on the door, so he knew he wasn't supposed to be there. "What are you doing here?" I demanded. "I had to go to the bathroom," he said. "Come on, you've got to be kidding," I retorted. "Who are you?"

"I work for the Mets," he told me. "You're outta here," I said. He became irate and told the media he was kicked out because he used the bathroom. The media printed his version, not mine, and it still irritates me every time I think about it.

I should have known how stories can get twisted after a previous bashing I had taken outside Tropicana Field when the media claimed I bullied a police officer and had "quite a temper tantrum" when he pulled over my wife for a traffic violation. According to news reports, I taunted the officer, yelling "Do you know who I am? I'm Vincent Naimoli, owner of the Devil Rays."

Here's the real story as I recall it. After Lenda was pulled over by a police officer, I tried to find out what happened. There was no bullying and no taunting and I believe there is a video taken from the police car to prove it, but the media apparently disregarded the tape of the incident which was in the police car. The officer claimed I was calling a lawyer, which wasn't true either. I never heard of the attorney they claimed I was calling. I was on the phone, but I was calling my friend, Rick Nafe, the stadium manager, to ask his advice.

I called the paper and demanded that they set things straight. But they never did. They had the video from the police car, so their story made no sense to me. You never get any retractions from them, because, in my opinion, the media manage perceptions according to their own agenda. I've tried, but it's useless. They make up anything they want about people, like the columnist and Notre Dame alum who wrote that I was not interested in the team winning. I was surprised because he knew me and knew of my passion for winning. I almost threw up when I read that. He equated our small payroll with apathy. I wonder what he thought when the team won the 2008 American League Championship with the second lowest payroll in the majors.

In the world of baseball, too many people believe money equals success.

I'm not one of them. It takes more than money. You need chemistry, good draft talent, skilled trades and a super-size helping of luck. I'd always been able to achieve success for companies by managing the cash carefully, trimming the fat and keeping my eye on the bottom line. It should have worked here.

That philosophy made the Naimoli name synonymous with "cheap." I was trying to do right by the team. Yet, I was lambasted because people thought I didn't put enough money into the team and therefore the team didn't win. Too bad they didn't know about the $30 million or so cash infusion and my partners reneging on their commitment.

But it's a Catch-22. If more fans attended the games, we would have more money to spend. You need money coming in to put money out. But my critics say I've got it backwards. Show 'em a winning team and the crowds will grow, they contend.

Certainly the fans didn't expect us to capture the World Series right away, I thought. Weren't they happy to root for a home team in the refurbished Tropicana Stadium, where it's always 72 degrees and 55 percent humidity? Here, they had a chance to see great baseball, even if it was played by the visiting team. There are limited number of places where you can see players like Derek Jeter, etc. and Tropicana Field is one of them.

Every time I went to the stadium, I realized how far we had come. We turned a partially built facility into a darn nice stadium. In 1996, $85 million was spent to modernize and finish it - we added 319,000 square feet of space, constructed an eight-story rotunda entrance and a 900-foot tropical-theme ceramic mosaic walkway. We added 200 points of purchase for a total of 290, built out the suites, made the concourses wider, bought a scoreboard, added ramps and seats for the handicapped and outfitted the locker rooms. It was the first major league park to have a cigar bar, which was fitting for the area, since Tampa is known as Cigar City.

Ever the engineer, I incorporated old-time details and modern comforts in the 15-month-long renovation. I had a plan for this indoor field of dreams: asymmetrical outfield dimensions, seats close to the

Rays win walk-off game

action, and a synthetic turf with dirt base paths and a rotundra reminiscent of Ebbetts Field. One of the things I'm most proud of is our home plate seats, which are 55 feet from home plate—that's closer than the pitcher is to home plate. If I had my druthers I'd have a retractable roof on the stadium. But the $200 million price brought me down to earth.

After all that work, the stadium was compared by some to a large warehouse. According to the Denver Post, "Dingy Tropicana Field, even with the ubiquitous cowbells clanging and some stadium improvements, simply doesn't supply a great baseball experience." It's ironic that a tour company went to 30 stadiums, including ours, and voted Tropicana Field the second-best facility.

The bloggers on TheTravelMavens.com got their digs in, too. "The Tampa Bay Rays play inside a domed park that feels somewhat like being in a basement recreation room, the walls and carpet damp from humidity. Tropicana Field is a dingy place with no windows."

Those criticisms mystified me. After all, we have 300 foot candles on the field, far more than most Major League fields, which have 250, the number I believe is mandated by Major League Baseball specs. If it was any brighter we'd need sunglasses.

Not all of the press was bad though. Rare, caring words in the press buoyed my spirits. It was an especially good day when I read Hal Bodley's MLB.com article in September 2008.

"This is about Naimoli, the much-maligned, often criticized father of baseball in the Tampa area," Bodley wrote. "He ran the franchise for its first eight rocky seasons. There were more bumps in the road than most owners endure and few successes, but without him, I'm convinced we wouldn't be celebrating the Rays atop American League East."

And kudos came from Gary Shelton of the St. Petersburg Times, who offered long-awaited accolades in 2008 when the Rays reached the World Series for the first time, beating the reigning champion Boston Red Sox 3-1 to win the American League

Welcome letter in the Inaugural game program

Tampa Bay Devil Rays Official Publi

DEVIL RAY
Vol.

March/April 1998

WELCOME TO THE NEW BALLPARK, ENJOY OUR INAUGURAL SEASON

On behalf of everyone in the Tampa Bay Devil Rays organization, I welcome you to Tropicana Field for our inaugural season in Major League Baseball.

This is an exciting time for all of us in the Tampa Bay area. As a community, we have supported big league baseball as far back as 1914, when Al Lang pioneered spring training in Florida by arranging for Branch Rickey's St. Louis Browns to train in St. Petersburg. Since then, for more than 83 years, the Tampa Bay area has served as baseball's unofficial spring training headquarters.

Now, with the debut of the Devil Rays, we take a huge, historic step — from spring time warm-ups to prime time action.

As a Tampa Bay area resident, I know first-hand this is one of the best sports towns in the country. I know we have all been waiting a long time to see big league baseball become a reality. And I know a lot of people have put in a tremendous amount of time and effort during the past 20-plus years to bring baseball to Tampa Bay. If it were earthly possible, I'd like to thank each one of you individually and shake your hand personally.

But, unfortunately, the huge number of people who participated in the effort make this impossible. Therefore, on behalf of our organization, please accept my heartfelt thanks to all of you for your efforts.

Now, as the Devil Rays begin this historic inaugural season, it is our goal to reward the community's effort, patience, loyalty and support in every way possible. And we look forward to sharing the fruits of everyone's hard work with you.

Under the expert direction of General Manager Chuck LaMar, one of the best minds in baseball, we have built, appropriately, an organization with a great emphasis on scouting and player development.

The team, under the guidance of Manager Larry Rothschild and his coaching staff, will play as hard as it can, on every play in every game. Larry, his coaches and our players are tough competitors. When they step onto the field, they care nothing about being an expansion franchise. They're out to win, and they'll be working as hard as they can to win as many games as possible.

A tremendous amount of effort went into transforming Tropicana Field into a state-of-the-art sports and fan-friendly entertainment facility. It took 17 months and $85 million, but we hope you agree that Tropicana Field is one of the most unique, enjoyable facilities in the country. You can now enjoy games in a ballpark that will be the talk of baseball.

Our goal in the 319,000-square-foot renovation and expansion was to make your experience at the ballpark as entertaining as possible. So, please, come to the games ready to explore. You'll see there is a lot for you and your friends, family and clients to enjoy before, during and after the game.

Finally, as we have during the past three years in preparing for this inaugural season, we will continue to solicit your input. We've worked hard at getting our team and ballpark ready. Now we want to continue to refine and enhance our efforts, and we want to make sure we're providing you with the highest-quality service possible.

You've been eager to share your thoughts with us in the past, and we've incorporated your feedback into our plans. I encourage you to continue providing your input. If you see me or any other member of the Devil Rays organization, feel free to pass along comments or suggestions. We not only want to know *what* you think; we *care* what you think.

It is my sincere hope that you enjoy today's game, the new Tropicana Field and this entire first season of Devil Rays Baseball. If it is true that good things come to those who wait, this and succeeding seasons will be ones to cherish for all of us.

Vince Naimoli

Vince Naimoli
Managing General Partner/CEO
Tampa Bay Devil Rays

MANAGING EDITOR
Rick Vaughn
Vice President of Public Relations

EDITOR
Mike Flanagan
Director of Publications

DIRECTOR OF PHOTOGRAPHY
Robert Rogers

DESIGNER
Raul Alsina
Assistant Director of Publications

CONTRIBUTING WRITERS
Don Lee
Tim Sweeney

VICE PRESIDENT OF SALES & MARKETIN
David I. Auker

DIRECTORS OF CORPORATE SALES
John Browne
Larry McCabe

MANAGERS OF SPONSORSHIP COORDINAT
Tammy Atmore
Jennifer Pajerski
Chris Trautmann

PRINTER
Feather Fine Printing & Direct Mail Service
Tampa

Devil Rays Magazine, the official publication of the Ta
Devil Rays, is published by the Tampa Bay Devil Rays
Club, Tropicana Field, One Tropicana Drive, St. Peters
33705. Its price includes Florida sales tax. De
Magazine, its logo and associated graphics are trade
the Tampa Bay Devil Rays, Ltd. All rights reserved.
1997. Tampa Bay Devil Rays, Ltd. For information abo
tising opportunities in *Devil Rays Magazine*, call 8
3137. Letters to *Devil Rays Magazine* should include t
address and home telephone number of the writer.
be mailed to Editor, *Devil Rays Magazine*, Tropicana F
Tropicana Drive, St. Petersburg, FL 33705. E-mail ma
to www.devilray.com.

University of Notre Dame du Lac

In recognition of his status as loyal alumnus in his service to God, country and fellowman, the University of Notre Dame and the Alumni Association confer upon its beloved son

Vincent J. Naimoli

in the **Golden Jubilee Year** of his graduation this

Special Citation

Rev. John Jenkins

President

Given at the
University of Notre Dame
Notre Dame, Indiana

June 6, 2009

Championship series. "It finally is time to appreciate Vince Naimoli. As an owner, he had a tight fist, a clumsy tongue and a habit of stepping on other people's toes… on the other hand, he brought baseball to Tampa Bay. He unlocked the building, he purchased the uniforms and he brought the ball… There should be a moment. There should be a cheer. Sometime tonight, between the anthem and the bottom of the Cracker Jack box, you should say thanks."

These words warmed my heart, but Gary Shelton still lambasted me for things I don't think are true. But still, when I read those tributes, I'm glad that I endured all the hardships to get the team here.

There were so many outstanding, memorable moments, like getting the very first "Bridging the Bay" award in 1996, which recognized me as the individual who had done the most to unite the citizens of Hillsborough and Pinellas counties. Baseball can unite people who never would have crossed paths otherwise.

And I still can vividly see double-jointed Andy Sonnanstine pitching for Kent State against Notre Dame and knowing he had to be a member of the Rays team. I encountered a little resistance, but I stuck to my ground and he was my one and only selection for the draft. He was slected in the 13th round of the June 2004 draft and he did me proud.

Pat Gillick, the general manager of four Major League Baseball teams, warned me not to fall in love with any of the players. But still, there were several I felt a kinship with, like 6 foot-4inch Rocco Baldelli, who reminded me of Joe DiMaggio. I befriended his parents during our chats at the games. Sonnanstine was another favorite, not only because of his talent but because I "adopted" him for the Rays family. Carl Crawford, who was named team MVP in 2004 and All Star Game MVP in 2009, is not only a talented athlete but a wonderful person. Trever Miller played his heart out, even when his thoughts drifted to his daughter who had a life-threatening disease. I always kept my distance from these players, but I rooted for them internally, probably just a little more than the other players. (There are others too, including Joe Kennedy, Bubba Trammell and Toby Hall, Scott Kazmir etc., and I apologize to those players I'm not mentioning).

Patch given at the
50th Notre Dame Reunion

My relationship with other baseball team owners was perplexing. In my life as a corporate owner, I was friends with other business owners. There was competition, but it never reached the extremes it did in baseball. "We're friends off the field, but enemies on the field," said George Steinbrenner, who along with his family have been good friends. Sometimes, it was a lonely life.

The fans were the true believers, though. I never heard a bad word from them. I often think back to a chance meeting with a fan in the mall. He congratulated me for bringing a team here. "It's a great accomplishment," he told me. "Why?" I asked him. "None of your players ever got into trouble," he told me. Now, that's a compliment.

Despite the support, I knew that I couldn't keep up the pace, so I was relieved when, in 2004, Stuart Sternberg bought out the other general partners and got 48 percent of the team,

I became chairman in 2006, then chairman emeritus in 2009. But I still have 100 percent of my stock, in fact I bought a little more. The perception is that I sold my stock, which I haven't. I haven't sold out on the team either. I still purchase season tickets. If I can't go to a game, I watch it on TV or make sure I get the score another way.

If I can't go to a game, I give my tickets to people I hope will become longtime fans. I believe if you go to one game, you will come back. I'm still one of the team's biggest fans.

It was strange not being at the helm of this great organization, but I adjusted. At least I could return to my money-making jobs and be out of the limelight, which I abhor. Extricating myself from the sharp jaws of the media was a plus.

I often recall a conversation I had with Gary Shelton in 2005. He pointed out that I was tied to the team and that I wasn't getting any younger. I thought about it and, although I didn't tell him at the time, he was right. I wasn't able to go on a Notre Dame alumni trip to China. I regretted that. And I had to forgo a military trip to Iwo Jima, an opportunity of a lifetime, to visit one of the most important battle sites of WWII. (In order to go there, you need permission of the Marine Corps commandant). There were many other adventures I missed as well.

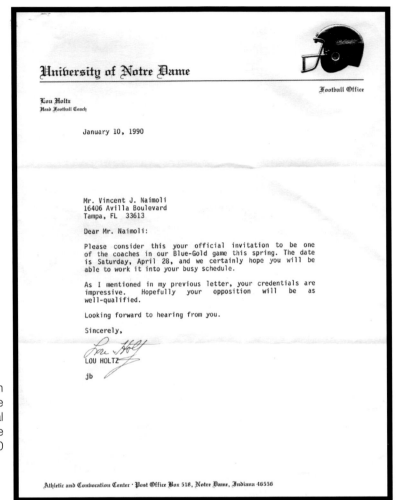

Invitation to Vince from Lou Holtz to be one of the coaches at the annual Blue-Gold game January, 1990

I may have missed opportunities but I never gave up my loyalty to my alma maters. In 2006, I gave $5 million toward a $24.7 million renovation of the Joyce Center arena at Notre Dame, used by the school's basketball and volleyball teams. The money went toward space for more than 750 spectators to sit, concessions and restrooms.

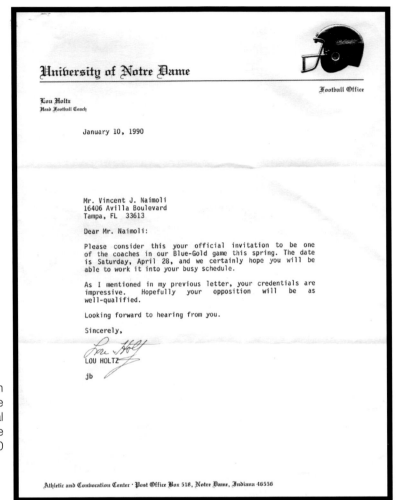

Invitation to Vince from Lou Holtz to be one of the coaches at the annual Blue-Gold game January, 1990

I may have missed opportunities but I never gave up my loyalty to my alma maters. In 2006, I gave $5 million toward a $24.7 million renovation of the Joyce Center arena at Notre Dame, used by the school's basketball and volleyball teams. The money went toward space for more than 750 spectators to sit, concessions and restrooms.

The next year I was happy to help Farleigh Dickinson University by donating $1 million for a baseball complex that included a 500-seat stadium. I also helped NJIT with a large gift for a practice facility.

These days, I am content to watch the Rays from the sidelines. I was intrigued in 2007 when the team took Devil out of its name and debuted new uniforms with two hues of blue and a bright yellow sunburst gleaming from the letter R. Kevin Costner, who starred in the baseball movie *Field of Dreams*, performed in downtown St. Petersburg with his band Modern West, to promote the event.

Vince with Lou Holtz

With these changes, I was slowly letting go of the baseball business. Life was eventful. Around that time, I was given the Outstanding Alumnus Award and an honorary doctorate of humane letters from New Jersey Institute of Technology. The Outstanding Alumnus event raised almost $400,000 for endowed scholarship funds for NJIT students, a cause close to my heart. I was also given the Charter Day Award from Farleigh Dickinson University. The proceeds from that event (we raised almost a half-million dollars!) are used for scholarships.

But the team was never far from my mind. And when it became an overnight success in its 12th season, clinching its first division title (the American League East) and then challenging the Philadelphia Phillies in the 2008 World Series, I was giddy with delight.

Long the underdogs, the team showed its worth. "Down to their last chance, the Tampa Bay Rays left no doubt they were World Series-worthy, after all," wrote the Associated Press. "Believe it: Baseball's doormats have arrived. Going from worst to first, the young Rays completed a stunning run to their first pennant."

Finally it all came together. Good luck, skilled trades and the players Mr. Sternberg and his colleagues signed and our nine years of first-round draft choices paid off.

At long last, the standing ovation came. "Mr. Baseball" Bob Stewart and I were front and center on the field before the first game of the World Series. He threw out the first pitch that October evening and the crowd roared. "We made it," I thought. And, I knew then that Mr. Sternberg and his colleagues were the right group to acquire the team and I compliment them on their skillful management of the team and wonderful trades they made.

Here we were, the team with the second-lowest payroll in the majors and we had outplayed the blue bloods of the East, Boston and the New York Yankees. That felt delicious. The Rays, once the butt of late-night television talk show jokes, showed them all.

Ironically, the World Series, which the Rays lost, was plagued by howling wind, single digit temperatures and rain. The crucial Game 5 was suspended in the fifth inning when a deluge made Philadelphia's Citizens Bank Park an unplayable swamp. "That was bad. That was probably the worst conditions I've ever played under in my life," Rays first baseman Carlos Pena was quoted as saying.

Behind the scenes, the team's traveling secretary, Jeffrey Ziegler, scrambled to find more than 60 hotel rooms for the players and staff who had checked out of their rooms, expecting to return to St. Pete that day. When the rain postponed the game, he did an amazing job of locating rooms and getting us back on track.

Ever the optimist, I believe that if we had won that rain-shortened game and gotten back to St. Petersburg for games 6 and 7, we would have won the World Series.

When we do win our first World Series championship, I'll be bursting with pride. And curious: Will people remember how it all began? How I helped make their dream come true?

Let's hope the truth will be known.

And now that my time and tribulations are over, I can go ***Beyond Baseball*** and move forward with new business ventures.

Remarks from Friends

Dr. Michael Adams

President
Fairleigh Dickinson University

*He is a powerful person for anyone
to aspire to be like.*

Dr. Robert Altenkirch

President
New Jersey Institute of Technology

*Vince works hard, is meticulous to detail,
and always timely.*

Anthony Ambrosio

Attorney at Law

*Vince is a man with a very generous spirit,
who has no airs, helps many, puts his money
where his mouth is... and leads by example.*

Dan Baldelli

(Rocco Baldelli's Father) Businessman

A man who lives and dies with every pitch.

Dan Beebe

Commissioner
Big 12 Conference

A kind and generous human being.

Gene Budig

Former President of the American League:

*His belief and persistence brought the miracle of the
Rays, a story of love, courage and determination. As an
owner of an American League club, Vince was tenacious
but fair, resolute but understanding. He was, without
question, a winner.*

Ray Chambers

CEO
Wesray/Entrenpenuer

I would call Vince Naimoli a "Renaissance Man," known for his business acumen, his entrepreneurial activities, his philanthropic contributions, his commitment to community service and, most importantly, his love of family.

Gene Deegan

Major General, USMC (retired)

It is easy to spot the Marine in Vince Naimoli - decisive, loyal and accountable with a clear focus on getting the job done right.

Bob Dilenschneider

Former President, Hill & Knowlton
Now President Dilenschneider Group

Vince is a fine man and a symbol of what a great American should be.

Jerry Colangelo

CEO, (retired)
Phoenix Suns and Arizona Diamondbacks

Good man, very sincere, and a hard working guy.

Rich DeVos

Co-Founder
Amway Corporation

Vince is a Grand Slam Winner

Rev. Theodore M. Hesburg, C.S.C.

President Emeritus
University of Notre Dame

I'm very grateful to him and I can say that what we've accomplished through the years is also part of his heritage because he made it happen.

Raymond L. Hollaway

VP/Anchor Hocking Corp. (retired)

I am very lucky to have met him and to have continued our friendship for thirty years.

Rev. John I. Jenkins, C.S.C.

President of the University of Notre Dame

Vince Namoli has been an accomplished leader in business and sport, and a generous contributor to the many communities of which he has been a part. The story of his life will be instructive and inspiring for us all.

Bob Martinez

Former Mayor of Tampa and Governor of Florida

Vince is not a spectator when work has to be done — he takes charge. That's why he's been successful in business, brought baseball to Tampa Bay when others failed, and made institutions of higher learning better through his service and philanthropy.

Bill McBride

Former head of Holland & Knight
Now, Partner of Barnett, Bolt, Kirkwood, Long & McBride

Vince has a great mind, he is generous, and as in his Marine Corps motto, Vince is "Semper Fidelis" — always faithful to his family.

John McDonald

CEO, JLM Industries:

He's an extremely likeable, fair, decent and generous man.

Lou Nanni

Vice President of University Relations at the University of Notre Dame

Vince is a man of great passion, whom Notre Dame is proud to claim as an alumnus and loyal son.

Philip Pumerantz, PhD

President
Western University of Health Sciences:

There's a description for men like Vince: 'good citizen.'

Jerry Reinsdorf

Owner of the Chicago White Sox
and Chicago Bulls:

*If it weren't for Vince Naimoli,
there would be no baseball in Tampa.*

Gen. Pete Schoomaker

US Army (retired), US Army Chief of Staff
Former Commander US Special Operations

*A fun character who has reached out and supported
the military community in the Tampa area during
times of peace and war.*

Jack Swarback

Director of Athletics
University of Notre Dame:

*Vince has the bright mind, competitive spirit and
generous heart that, together, enable a person to
make a difference in the world – and Vince has
certainly made a difference.*

Ronald L. Vaughn

President
University of Tampa

*Vince is a smart man, always impressing
me with his attention to both "big picture"
strategy and tactical issues as well as small
details, which is why he is a very successful
business man.*

Dick Vitale

Sportscaster, ESPN

*Vince Namoli is a man who has a passion,
an incredible passion for whatever he does.*

Steve Waters

Partner
Compass Partners

*Vince's determination and loyalty to
his friends is unsurpassed.*

John R. Willis

Partner
Wills & Stein

*He is truly an insightful and thoughtful
leader as well as a heck of a good guy.*

Don Zimmer

Major League Baseball icon

*He helped bring baseball here. We should
all remember that.*

Gen. Tony Zinni

USMC, (retired)
Former Commander, Central Command

*Vince Naimoli is a true friend
and a remarkable man with a great
American story*

Appendix

RAYS CHRONOLOGY

MARCH 9, 1995
At a meeting in West Palm Beach, Fla., baseball owners officially welcome the Tampa Bay Devil Rays and Arizona Diamondbacks as the 13th and 14th expansion teams in major league history by a vote of 28-0.

APRIL 27, 1995
The Rays and the City of St. Petersburg agree on a 30-year lease for the team to play their home games at the ThunderDome.

JULY 19, 1995
Chuck LaMar is named Rays Senior Vice President of Baseball Operations and General Manager.

SEPTEMBER 26, 1995
The Rays sign their first player — pitcher Adam Sisk, a 6-4 righthander from Edison Community College in Fort Myers, Fla.

MAY 7, 1996
The Rays announce they will become the first team in the modern era to host spring training in their home city in 1998. The National League's St. Louis Cardinals will leave after training in St. Petersburg since 1946.

JUNE 3, 1996
The Rays begin their first mini-camp as 24 players, all minor league free agents signed before the June draft, assemble at the Huggins-Stengel complex in St. Petersburg under the watchful eye of the Rays coaching staff directed by Field Coordinator Tom Foley.

JUNE 4, 1996
Outfielder and first baseman Paul Wilder becomes the Rays first-ever draft pick as the team participates in its first June Draft. Rays Managing Partner Vince Naimoli announces the selection while in the team's "war room" at the Stouffer-Vinoy Resort in St. Petersburg. The Rays eventually select 97 the players, the fifth-highest total ever taken in the 32-year history of the June Draft.

JUNE 18, 1996
The first game involving Rays players is held at Skylands Park in Augusta, N.J., where the visiting Hudson Valley Renegades, the Rays co-operative team in the Class-A New York-Penn League with the Texas Rangers, face the New Jersey Cardinals. Catcher Chris Anderson, the Rays 66th round draft choice from Southeast Oklahoma State University, delivers an RBI single in the second inning for the first hit ever by a Rays player.

JUNE 19, 1996
The first Rays game is played. A Gulf Coast League record crowd of 7,582 are on hand at Al Lang Stadium as the GCL Devil Rays host their Yankee counterparts. A 10-1 loss can't dim the festive atmosphere nor the unbridled affection that is showered down on the young Rays. The game was carried live by News Radio 970 WFLA and SportsChannel Florida. Eighteen-year-old righthander Pablo Ortega throws the first Rays pitch (a ball).

JUNE 19, 1996
Butte infielder Jim Kerr hits the first home run in Rays history in the Copper Kings' Pioneer League opener against Idaho Falls.

JUNE 20, 1996
The first win in the history of the Rays organization, a 4-3 triumph over the Gulf Coast League Astros. Eighteen year-old Jose Rodriguez from the Dominican Republic gets the win.

OCTOBER 3, 1996
Tropicana Field is born. The Rays and Tropicana Dole Beverages North America of nearby Bradenton, Fla., announce an agreement to rename the ThunderDome. The City of St. Petersburg receives more than $13 million as a result of the agreement.

OCTOBER 7, 1996
Vince Naimoli and St. Petersburg Mayor David Fischer preside over the official groundbreaking ceremony for a 15-month, $63 million renovation of Tropicana Field.

JANUARY 16, 1997
The Rays are voted into the American League by a 28-2 count among MLB owners, becoming the Junior Circuit's 15th franchise. The decision is announced at owner's meetings in Phoenix, Ariz.

RAYS CHRONOLOGY

APRIL 21, 1997
The Rays sign pitcher Rolando Arrojo, the ace of the Cuban National Team.

SEPTEMBER 9, 1997
The Rays organization celebrates the first championship in its short history as Manager Bill Evers' St. Petersburg Rays beat Vero Beach, 5-1, at Al Lang Field to win the Class-A Florida State League Championship.

OCTOBER 15, 1997
MLB approves a resolution creating a 16-team National League and a 14-team American League for the 1998 season, meaning the Rays will be located in the AL East Division.

NOVEMBER 7, 1997
Florida Marlins Pitching Coach Larry Rothschild is named the first Rays Manager.

NOVEMBER 11, 1997
The Rays acquire outfielder Mike Kelly from the Cincinnati Reds for a player to be named later. Kelly becomes the first player to be added to the 40-man major league roster. This is the Rays first-ever trade involving a major league player.

NOVEMBER 18, 1997
The Rays select 35 players in the Major League Expansion Draft. The Rays select LHP Tony Saunders from the Florida Marlins with the first pick in the draft.

DECEMBER 9, 1997
The Rays sign free agent third baseman Wade Boggs.

FEBRUARY 15, 1998
The Rays first major league spring training camp opens. Fifty-one players, including 41 pitchers, take the field at 9:35 a.m. at the Rays Spring Training Complex, Busch Complex. It was a three-hour workout and the day also was marked by the team's first injury as catcher Cesar Devarez suffered a dislocated left knee cap.

FEBRUARY 26, 1998
The first spring training game involving Rays major leaguers takes place. The Rays beat Florida State University in what will be the last game at Al Lang Stadium. The next day the facility is renamed Florida Power Park, Home of Al Lang Field. The Rays use 30 players in the win over Florida State and rally from a 3-1 deficit with a five-run 8th inning. Matt White is the Rays starting pitcher and Jason Johnson gets the win. Quinton McCracken leads off the game for the Rays with a single to right field.

MARCH 2, 1998
Tampa Bay wins its first major league spring training game, 6-2 over visiting Kansas City. Lefty Ryan Karp is the winner as the Rays win it with a four-run rally in the 7th inning.

MARCH 27, 1998
In the first game at Tropicana Field, the Rays beat Atlanta, 5-0, in an exhibition game that draws 26,519. Rolando Arrojo beats Tom Glavine and Russ Mormon hits the first home run, a 380-foot shot to left-center.

MARCH 31, 1998
It all begins. The Rays lose to the Detroit Tigers 11-6 in Tampa Bay's first official major league game before what remains the largest crowd in Rays history – 45,369. Hall of Famers Ted Williams, Stan Musial, Al Lopez and Monte Irvin throw out the ceremonial first pitches. Wilson Alvarez throws the first pitch in Rays history, a ball to Detroit's Brian Hunter.

APRIL 1, 1998
"Say hello to victory, Tampa Bay," says Rays radio voice Paul Olden as the Rays win for the first time, 11-8 over Detroit. Cuban ace Rolando Arrojo is the winner in his major league debut.

APRIL 11, 1998
The Rays record their first road win, a 5-1 victory at Chicago White Sox behind the sterling pitching of Chicago-area native Rick Gorecki.

APRIL 19, 1998
Tampa Bay wins 6-0 at Anaheim to go 10-6, thus becoming the first expansion team ever to be four games over .500 at any point in their inaugural season.

JUNE 21, 1998
Raymond, the team's mascot, debuts prior to the Rays-Red Sox game at Tropicana Field.

RAYS CHRONOLOGY

AUGUST 7, 1999
Wade Boggs homers at Tropicana Field off Cleveland's Chris Haney for his 3,000th career hit. Boggs is the first to reach the milestone with a home run.

APRIL 7, 2000
The Rays host the Cleveland Indians at Tropicana Field. It is the first professional baseball game played on FieldTurf, artificial grass that has all the characteristics of natural grass.

AUGUST 10, 2000
Hudson Valley righthander Doug Waechter throws the first 9-inning no-hitter in the history of the Rays organization. Waechter beats Pittsfield (Mets) at Hudson Valley.

APRIL 18, 2001
Hal McRae is named the second manager in club history replacing Larry Rothschild.

OCTOBER 28, 2002
Tampa native Lou Piniella is named manager of the Rays.

MARCH 30, 2004
The Rays open the major league season at the Tokyo Dome in Japan with an 8-3 win over the New York Yankees in front of 55,000 and a national TV audience.

JUNE 26, 2004
The Rays beat the Marlins, 6-4, and become the first team in history to climb over .500 after being 18 or more games below .500. The Rays were 10-28 on May 19, but 26-7 in their next 33 games to get to 36-35.

OCTOBER 6, 2005
Stuart Sternberg becomes the principal owner of the Rays and takes control of the operation of the organization. Matt Silverman is named club president. That same day, Sternberg announces that the team will offer free parking at all Rays home games next season making the Rays the only Major League Baseball franchise to offer free parking on all team-owned lots.

OCTOBER 26, 2005
The Rays and concessionaire Centerplate announce a change in its food policy effective for the 2006 season. For the first time in team history, fans will be permitted to bring food and certain drinks into Tropicana Field for Rays home games.

NOVEMBER 3, 2005
The Rays announce that Andrew Friedman will oversee the Rays baseball operations efforts and that former National League Executive of the Year Gerry Hunsicker would be brought on to assist Friedman.

NOVEMBER 15, 2005
The Rays name Angels Bench Coach Joe Maddon as the fourth manager in team history.

DECEMBER 2005
The Rays begin a $10 million refurbishment of Tropicana Field. These improvements are all designed to heighten the fan experience. Bathrooms are renovated, 35,000 seats are cleaned and painted, concrete walls are covered with stucco and drywall, the suite and club sections are upgraded, a new upscale club is added along the first base side concourse, new directional signs and outdoor awnings are added and a new sound system is installed. Concourses are converted into interactive fun zones for all fans.

FEBRUARY 23, 2006
The Ted Williams Museum and Hitters Hall of Fame opens a new location at Tropicana Field.

JULY 21, 2006
The Rays unveil the Rays Touch Tank, an exciting new addition to Tropicana Field featuring 30 cownose rays from the Florida Aquarium. The experience is free to all fans attending home games.

SEPTEMBER 20, 2006
The Rays and the Board of County Commissioners of Charlotte County, Fla., formally sign a 20-year agreement for the Rays to conduct Spring Training at a renovated Charlotte Sports Park beginning in February 2009.

RAYS CHRONOLOGY

JANUARY 2007
For the second consecutive year, improvements are made to Tropicana Field. The changes — estimated at $8 million and paid by the club — include a new look to the exterior of the stadium and a state-of-the-art 36'-by-64' full-color scoreboard. Three other smaller, but cutting edge technology scoreboards are also to be added. This round of improvements extends to the playing surface. The FieldTurf surface installed before the 2000 season is replaced by the very latest FieldTurf product.

MAY 15-17, 2007
In another step toward creating a more regional presence for the team, the Rays play the first regular season major league games ever in Orlando and sweep the Texas Rangers in a three-game series at The Ballpark at Disney's Wide World of Sports Complex.

JULY 10, 2007
Carl Crawford becomes the first Rays player to hit a home run in an All-Star Game when he delivers a solo blast off Milwaukee's Francisco Cordero in the 78th All-Star Classic at San Francisco.

NOVEMBER 8, 2007
The organization launches new uniforms, new colors, a new icon and a new name — the Rays. The re-branding effort begins with a fashion show in downtown St. Petersburg and a free concert by Hollywood's Kevin Costner and his band Modern West. Approximately 7,000 attend the event at Straub Park.

JULY 15, 2008
Rays lefty Scott Kazmir picks up the win in the 79th All-Star Game at Yankee Stadium as the American League prevails, 4-3 in 15 innings. The victory winds up giving the Rays the home-field advantage in the World Series.

AUGUST 10, 2008
The Rays win their 71st game at Seattle in their 117th game, setting the franchise record for wins in a season.

SEPTEMBER 20, 2008
The Rays defeat Minnesota, 7-2, at Tropicana Field in front of a national TV audience and clinch their first postseason appearance.

SEPTEMBER 26, 2008
The Rays lose at Detroit, 6-4, but clinch the AL East title when Boston loses to the Yankees, 19-8.

OCTOBER 19, 2008
Matt Garza starts it and rookie David Price finishes it as the Rays win Game 7 of the ALCS, 3-1 to clinch the American League pennant in front of 40,473 at Tropicana Field.

OCTOBER 22, 2008
The Rays host the Phillies in their first World Series game becoming just the second team in major league history to compete in the World Series the year after having the worst record in the majors.

NOVEMBER 10, 2008
Rays third baseman Evan Longoria wins the AL Rookie of the Year Award, becoming the first Ray to win a national BBWAA award. Two days later, Joe Maddon becomes the second when he is voted AL Manager of the Year.

HISTORY OF BASEBALL IN ST. PETERSBURG

This year marks the 90th season in which Major League Baseball has had a presence in St. Petersburg, dating back to February 27, 1914 when the St. Louis Browns opened spring training workouts in the Sunshine City.

With the Rays moving their spring home to Charlotte County, this is the first year St. Petersburg has been without a spring training team since 1945 when travel restrictions during World War II prohibited teams from traveling south for the spring. Nonetheless, more major league spring training games have been played in St. Petersburg than in any other city.

Nine teams have trained in St. Petersburg: the St. Louis Browns (1914), Philadelphia Phillies (1915-18), Boston Braves (1922-37), New York Yankees (1925-42; 1946-50; 1952-61), St. Louis Cardinals (1938-42; 1946-97), New York Giants (1951), New York Mets (1962-87), Baltimore Orioles (1993-95), and the Rays (1998-2008).

In 1910, a former Pittsburgh laundry owner named Al Lang moved to St. Petersburg to benefit his health. He soon became interested in the local economy and focused on trying to help the sagging tourism industry. As a baseball fan, he believed the answer was to attract a major league team to St. Petersburg for Spring Training.

Lang convinced the St. Louis Browns, under General Manager Branch Rickey, to move to St. Petersburg in 1914. A baseball committee, formed to attract a major league team to the city, raised $20,000 to buy a large tract of land for a ballpark. The site chosen for the field was Coffee Pot Bayou in St. Petersburg, where a 2,000-seat grandstand was built.

The first game between two major league teams in St. Petersburg took place on March 27, 1914 as the Grapefruit League was established. The Browns hosted the Chicago Cubs, who were training in Tampa and made the trip by steamboat across Tampa Bay. The Cubs won, 3-2. James Leslie (Hippo) Vaughn was the winning pitcher for the Cubs as an estimated 4,000 looked on.

The resourceful Lang helped engineer a new ballpark, Waterfront Park, located at the approximate site where the parking lot for Progress Energy Park, home of Al Lang Field is today. A new arrival, the Boston Braves, christened the new park in 1922. The Yankees joined the Braves in St. Petersburg in 1925. They would stay until 1962, when the Casey Stengel and the expansion New York Mets moved in and the Yankees went to Fort Lauderdale.

When the Boston Braves left for Bradenton in 1937, the St. Louis Cardinals came to St. Petersburg the following year and would stay 57 of the next 60 years, missing only the war years.

Minor league baseball in St. Petersburg began in 1920 when the St. Pete Saints entered the Florida State League. By 1922, the Saints had won a FSL crown.

There was one other professional league in St. Petersburg prior to the Rays arrival in 1998. The Senior Professional Baseball Association, a league of former major leaguers who were 35 years of age or older, sprang up for one season, 1989-90. The St. Pete Pelicans were the first and only league champions.

The expansion Mets take the field at Huggins-Stengel Complex in St. Petersburg for Spring Training in 1962.

Photo courtesy of St. Petersburg Museum of History

TROPICANA FIELD

Skip Milos

▶ Originally named the Florida Suncoast Dome, Tropicana Field's 1.1 million square feet include unique design features and fan amenities found nowhere else in the major leagues.

▶ The venue was opened to the public on March 3, 1990, at a cost of $138 million. It became the ThunderDome in 1993 with the arrival of the area's National Hockey League expansion franchise, the Tampa Bay Lightning. It was renamed Tropicana Field on Oct 4, 1996, in accordance with a naming rights agreement between the Rays and Bradenton's Tropicana Dole Beverages North America.

▶ The current capacity is 36,048 with the portion of the upper deck tarped. Without the tarps the capacity increases to 41,810.

▶ Over 2006-07, the Rays invested more than $18 million on improvements to Tropicana Field including the creation of the Whitney Bank Club, major improvements to the interior of the park, the installation of new video boards and a sound system and the addition of the Ted Williams Museum and Hitters Hall of Fame located in Center Field Street.

▶ Tropicana Field is also the world's only professional sports facility that features live rays. The Rays Touch Tank opened in 2006, and is located just behind the right-center field wall. Through a unique partnership with the Florida Aquarium, there are over 20 cownose rays that fans can touch and feed throughout the game. The 10,000-gallon tank is sponsored by the Pinellas County Visitors Bureau and Florida-Beaches.com and is one of the 10 largest in the United States.

▶ Tropicana Field is the only major league `park to feature an artificial surface and all-dirt base paths. Only four other artificial turf ballparks have ever featured all-dirt base paths: Houston's Astrodome (1966-71); San Francisco's Candlestick Park in 1971; Pittsburgh's Three Rivers Stadium in the early '70s; and, most recently, St. Louis' Busch Stadium (1970-76).

▶ The Rays first installed FieldTurf in 2000 becoming the first pro baseball team to play on the top-of-the-line synthetic playing surface. In February 2007, the Rays installed FieldTurf's latest upgrade becoming first baseball facility in the world to feature the company's unique duo filament system.

▶ Tropicana Field features the world's second-largest cable-supported domed roof (Georgia Dome is the largest). It's made of six acres of translucent, Teflon-coated fiberglass and it virtually supports itself with 180 miles of cables connected by struts. Opposing forces of tension and compression keep the roof in an arc. Tropicana Field's roof is slanted at a 6.5-degree angle, dropping from 225 feet above second base to 85 feet at the center field wall. The slanted roof reduced the overall construction costs and decreased the volume of air under the dome by 16.8 million cubic feet. Accordingly, that reduced the amount of air that requires climate control treatment. It is built to withstand wind of up to 115 miles per hour.

▶ Though originally built for baseball, there have been 16 other sports and competitive events held there. These include hockey, basketball, football, sprint car racing, gymnastics, soccer, tennis, weightlifting, ping-pong, karate, motorcycle racing, equestrian events, track and figure skating.

▶ The facility was also home to the 1999 NCAA Basketball Final Four, featuring Duke, Ohio State, Michigan State and eventual-champion Connecticut. The largest crowd to date - 47,150 - appeared at the Aug 11, 1990, concert featuring New Kids on the Block.

Profile

Vincent J. Naimoli

(Chairman, and Chairman Emeritus, Tampa Bay Rays)

The man who secured Tampa Bay's long-awaited Major League Baseball franchise on March 9, 1995, continues to work as hard as anyone to build a championship team.

Taking the torch from a long line of community leaders, in 1991 Naimoli accepted the challenge of bringing the National Pastime to the region. Summoning the grit and problem-solving savvy that took him from a humble start in Paterson, N.J., to an NROTC scholarship at Notre Dame, two master's degrees, the engineering and business worlds, and legendary status as a corporate turnaround specialist, he rallied civic and financial backers to the baseball cause. Naimoli had the ticket-buying public behind him, too, and on March 31, 1998, a $250-million-a-year economic entity began play at Tropicana Field.

Naimoli forged a naming-rights deal with Tropicana Products that will enable St. Petersburg to receive payments of more than $13 million over the life of the contract, and he and fellow Rays owners paid for improvements at The Trop and the club's spring stadium, Florida Power Park, home of Al Lang Field. He insisted that Tropicana Field's design reflect baseball traditions, among them asymmetrical outfield dimensions, seats close to the action, and dirt base paths.

Ever the engineer, he let innovation enhance that traditional feel by arranging the purchase of a revolutionary grasslike playing surface, FieldTurf, for the air-conditioned dome before the 2000 season, earning unanimous approval from the league, players, fans and media. Old-time details blend with modern comforts to create a stadium ranked second in the majors by a group of fans who watched games at every one on their 30 Ballpark Millennium Tour.

While building a franchise from within, Naimoli also has focused on the game's welfare. In addition to serving on MLB committees, he was named in January 1999 to the Blue Ribbon Task Force on Baseball Economics, whose recommendations addressed longstanding problems.

As CEO of Anchor Industries International, Naimoli was voted 1995 Florida Entrepreneur of the Year in the "turnaround" category. In 1999 he joined former First Lady and current Senator Hillary Clinton, Senator John Glenn and Chief Justice of the Supreme Court William Rehnquist in receiving the Ellis Island Medal of Honor from the National Ethnic Coalition of Organizations. He also has served on financial and athletic committees at alma mater Notre Dame, and also served as named Chairman of the Notre Dame College Business Administration Advisory Council. In addition, he chaired the University of Tampa Board of Trustees, now Chairman Emeritus, serves on the board of overseers at New Jersey Institute of Technology where he earned an M.S.M.E., and serves on the board at Fairleigh Dickinson University (where he earned an M.B.A. magna cum laude) before completing Harvard Business School's advanced management program in 1974. In the community, Naimoli has received numerous honors for service, including the first Bridging the Bay Award in 1996 and the NJIT outstanding alumnus award in 2007.

One of four children of a second-generation Italian immigrant who worked for the New York subway system and became a self-taught stationary engineer, Naimoli graduated from Notre Dame in 1959 out of Paterson Central High School. He still attends Fighting Irish football games with his wife, Lenda, who retired as an Eastern Airlines flight attendant after 24 years and who has an identical twin, Mrs. J.E. (Glenda) Young. He has four daughters, Christine, an Arizona State graduate; Tory Ann Jarvis, Stephens College and Kellogg Graduate School alumna; Alyson, a Notre Dame graduate; and Lindsey, a Notre Dame graduate, presently studying for a Doctor of Veterinarian Medicine degree at Western University; three Jarvis grandchildren, Jack Burke, Matthew Vincent and William Joseph, and one Dorfman grandchild, Enzo Maxmillian.

POSITION HELD

Business Description

Tampa Bay Rays (Private) Founder, Managing General Partner/CEO & Chairman (Principal Owner)	Major League Baseball Franchise.
Anchor Industries International Inc. and Naimoli Business Enterprises Chairman, President & CEO	Holding/Investment Companies
Anchor Glass Container Corporation ($1.2 Billion)	Manufacturer of glass containers,

Founder, Chairman, President & CEO

Harding Service Corporation – Holding Entity
Company for
Chairman/CEO,

Electrolux Corporation ($500 million)
Chairman, President & CEO

The Regina Company ($300 million)
Chairman/CEO

Doehler-Jarvis, Inc. ($300 million)
Chairman/CEO

Ladish Co., Inc. ($250 million)
President & CEO

Harvard Industries, Inc. ($900 million)
Chairman, President & CEO

Tampa Bay Lightning (Private)
Interim Chief Executive Officer

Allegheny Beverage Corp. ($150 million)
President/COO

closures, plastic containers and
specialty glass.

Management Services

LBO firm (Wesray Corp.).

Manufacturer/Marketer of high quality
cleaning machines.

Manufacturer/Marketer of cleaning
machines.

Manufacturer of precisionautomotive/
truck components (aluminum die-
cast).

Manufacturer of high Chairman,
tech aerospace, aircraft, nuclear and
industrial parts.
Titanium and other exotic materials).

Manufacturer of varied
line of automotive/truck components.

National Hockey League Franchise.

Second Largest Pepsi Franchise
Holder.

Continental Can Company ($5 billion)
Vice President/General Manager
M/A, Planning and Engineering Positions.

Various Manufacturing, Marketing,
Sales,

INDUSTRY EXPERIENCE

Crisis Management positions began as Director or Consultant, then asked to become CEO
by either equity holders or banks.

Packaging, Automotive/truck, Aerospace, Industrial and Consumer Products, Professional
Sports Franchise Industry, Entertainment, LBO Firms, M/A, etc.

SPECIAL AWARDS (Partial List)

Ellis Island Medal of Honor

Florida Entrepreneur of the Year

Notre Dame Engineering Honor Award

Urban League Chairman's Award

Fairleigh Dickinson University (FDU)

Northwood University

National Multiple Sclerosis Hope Award
NJIT Outstanding Alumnus Award
FDU Outstanding Alumnus Award
(2009)

Council of Independent Colleges/
   C.H.I.E.F.
(Champion of Higher Independent
   Education in FL)
Boys & Girls Club
   Man of the Year Award
Jewish National Fund
   Tree of Life Award
Pinnacle AwardBusiness
   Hall of Fame Award
Outstanding Business Leaders Award
   Tampa Citizen of the Year Award
Tampa Bay Bridge Builder Award
FDU Charter Day Honoree
NJIT Honorary Doctorate Degree

PRESENT DIRECTORSHIPS

Strategic Materials, Inc.
University of Notre Dame/ College of
Outback Bowl (Emeritus)
Northwood University OBL Executive Committee

Engineering Advisory Council
University of Notre Dame/ Business
Advisory Council**

Notre Dame President's Advisory Council

PAST DIRECTORSHIPS

JLM Industries, Inc.
Simplicity Pattern Co., Inc.
Resorts International, Inc.
National Gypsum Company
Players International, Inc.
Anchor Glass Container Corporation
Dyersburg Fabrics Corporation
Kohlbern Schmidt/DJ Joint Venture
Harvard Industries, Inc.
University of Tampa, Board of Trustees***
New Jersey Institute of Technology
Board of Overseers

Heekin Can Company
Six Flags Corporation
JP Petroleum
New River Industries, Inc.
Wm. Carter Company
Ally and Gargano
Florida Progress Corporation
Russell-Stanley Corporation

**Past Chairman of the Board
*** Former Trustee, then Chairman of the Board, now Chairman Emeritus

SPECIAL RELATIONSHIPS

KEY GOVERNMENT CONTACTS:

Major League Baseball Legislative Affairs Committee; various congressional personal contacts including Congressman McCollum, Keller, Wexler, Young, Bilirakis, Davis and Senators Graham, Nelson, Mack and Bradley.

SPECIAL INTERNATIONAL AFFILIATIONS/CONTACTS:

Former Director – Kohlbern-Schmidt joint venture (Germany); affiliation with Hutchinson Division of Total Oil Corp. (France); Toyota Motor Corp. (Japan); Vitro Corp., Group Alpha and Peralta Industries (Mexico) and other various Mexican, Japanese, Dominican and Venezuelan contacts.

Past Member – Major League Baseball International Committee and Sub-Committee on World Baseball Classic, Legislative Affairs Committee, Equal Opportunity Committee. Past member – Major League Baseball Blue Ribbon Committee.

DOMESTIC AFFILIATIONS/CONTACTS:

Contacts include owners of Major League Sports franchises, many of whom are CEO's of major entities, various investment banking contacts, including Salomon Smith Barney, Morgan Stanley Dean Witter, Wachovia, Bank of America, Dillon Reed, Bear Stearns, Vestar Capital Corp., Compass Partners; Trust Company of the West, Fidelity Corp., J.P. Morgan-Chase and Citicorp.

Involvement with Paul Volker, George Will, Senator George Mitchell and Richard Levin (President of Yale) while serving on Major League Baseball Blue Ribbon Committee.

Member- Florida Council of 100 (Approved by Governor of Florida)

TRADE ASSOCIATIONS

Can Makers Institute (Past Member);   MLB Business/Political Forum
Glass Packaging Institute (Past Member).

POTENTIAL ROLES

PORTFOLIO COMPANIES AND NEW ACQUISITIONS

Available for further involvement which includes anything from Non-Executive Chairman, Chief Executive Officer for a period of time, a member of the Board of Directors, or as a Consultant.

Go to Work and Smile

If you are poor-work.

If you are rich-continue to work.

If you are happy-keep right on working.

Idleness gives room for doubt and fears.

If disappointments come-work.

If sorrow overwhelms you and loved ones seem not true-work.

If health is threatened-work.

When faith falters and reasons fail-just work.

When dreams are shattered and hope seems dead-work.

Work as if your life was in peril. It really is.

Whatever happens or matters-work.

Work is the greatest material remedy available.

Work will cure both mental and physical afflictions.

From "Silent Partner"

Plaque given to Vince by a friend

For more information, contact:

Vince Naimoli

RAYS
One Tropicana Drive
St. Petersburg, Florida 33705

727.825.3137

www.raysbaseball.com

www.vincenaimoli.com